T0146683

# WOK & GO

## FROM YO-YO FAT
## TO HEALTHY SLIM

Frances Wood-Parker

authorHOUSE®

*AuthorHouse™*
*1663 Liberty Drive*
*Bloomington, IN 47403*
*www.authorhouse.com*
*Phone: 1-800-839-8640*

*Cover design by Frances Wood-Parker*

*Published by AuthorHouse    11/06/2014*

*ISBN: 978-1-4969-5276-9 (hc)*
*ISBN: 978-1-4969-4168-8 (sc)*
*ISBN: 978-1-4969-4167-1 (e)*

*Library of Congress Control Number: 2014916967*

# CONTENTS

# INTRODUCTION

Have you ever heard yourself and others say: 'I've gained and lost hundreds of pounds over my lifetime and now weigh more than ever?' For fifty years of my life I was either 'on' a diet losing weight, or 'off' a diet gaining weight. After years of being a victim of the yo-yo diet syndrome, I simply gave up and started eating anything and everything I wanted. Naturally my weight skyrocketed and I felt helpless to do anything about it. Most of my life I have struggled with health issues including allergies, asthma, lung and sinus infections, hypoglycemia, constipation, painful gas, yeast and parasite infections, mental fog, extreme fatigue, and painful joints.

Seven years ago when I turned sixty, I was more than sixty pounds heavier than I am today. A size 2X top was a tight fit then; today I wear a small top and a medium pant. I am 5 feet 2 inches in height with a small bone structure. Before I changed my eating habits to the ones recommended in this book, my knees were inflamed and sore from multiple old injuries. Standing for any length of time was excruciatingly painful, and I was afraid I was headed for a life in a wheel chair. In addition, the mental fog with which I was living made me feel more like ninety than sixty. When I went to my primary care doctor, Dr. Craig Reese, D.C., P.C. of Boulder, Colorado his diagnosis was that of systemic Mycological Syndrome (a yeast/mold/ fungal infection). He put me on The Yeast Diet, and I have stayed on it ever since. I was successfully healed of this syndrome with pharmaceutical-grade food supplements and strictly adhering to this eating strategy. Ironically, after spending most of my life with weight loss being my goal, I attained successful weight loss and maintenance as a side effect of sticking to a diet which helped cure an infection.

The Yeast Diet is in alignment with the dietary recommendations of two medical doctors: (1) Dr. Mark Hyman, author of *The Blood Sugar Solution*, a book and a presentation on television through PBS; and (2) Dr. David Perlmutter, a Board Certified Neurologist and a Fellow on the Board of the American College of Nutrition. His book is entitled *Grain Brain* and he also has a presentation available on PBS entitled *Brain Change*. Dr. Hyman focuses on the reversal and prevention of Diabetes. Dr. Perlmutter is concerned with the reversal of various brain disorders, especially the prevention of Alzheimer's. This guide is intended to bridge the information contained in both books and to share my personal experience with the Yeast Diet.

By staying on this eating regimen for more than seven years, I have prevented my Reactive Hypoglycemia from progressing to insulin-dependent, Type II Diabetes. I am hopeful it will also stave off Type III Diabetes, now classified as Dementia. When I became aware of the scientific information contained in Drs. Hyman and Perlmutter's books, their dietary recommendations were already incorporated into my daily diet. When I first discovered Dr. Perlmutter's *Brain Change* presentation on PBS, I adjusted my 83-year-old husband's diet slightly to be in alignment with his program. In doing so his symptoms of Dementia and Parkinson Syndrome improved within several months. Although he didn't need to lose any weight, he certainly needed to improve his brain function. The removal of sugar, gluten, and carbohydrates and the addition of avocado, nuts and other brain-healthy oils have definitely made an improvement in both disorders.

This book was created from my personal, daily journal which was seven years in the making. It incorporates all the aspects of what it takes to lose excess weight and keep it off in a very healthy way. This book addresses (1) ways to re-program your mind for success; (2) a detailed account of the kitchen equipment that will streamline the process; (3) a method which combines meal planning and grocery shopping with one single piece of paper; (4) cooking techniques that will produce quick and delicious meals; (5) behavioral tips on how to maneuver through social and other situations so you can adhere to the diet plan which will give you a slim and healthy body; (6) a discussion of sugar addiction and how to break it; and (7) why we now have an obesity epidemic.

Have you ever wondered when, why, and how America became a country with an obesity epidemic? There is an in-depth discussion about this subject. I have first-hand knowledge because it is the story of my life. It is my intention to empower the reader by exploring this historical information so that history does not necessarily need to repeat itself. This guide will give, in great detail, the psychological, behavioral, and addictive challenges I have encountered over five decades. I was a victim of the yo-yo diet syndrome, sugar addiction, feelings of defectiveness, and sickly. This guide shows how I made the lifestyle change to eliminate all of them.

I was raised in a time and culture where sugar, in every form imaginable, was at its center. Throughout my childhood, and until I reached the age of sixty, the daily consumption of sugar and complex carbohydrates was the center of my world. Everyone who consumes sugar does not necessarily become addicted to it. Just as many social drinkers can have an occasional alcoholic beverage without becoming an alcoholic, there are some people who can eat sugar without becoming addicted. Nevertheless, sugar is an appetite stimulant. In many cultures fruit or a sweet liqueur is served before a meal to stimulate the appetite. I believe anyone would agree that for those who are attempting to lose weight, the last thing they need is a potentially addictive, appetite stimulant!

Brain disorders such as Dementia, ADHD, Depression, and Alzheimer's are also quickly rising in our population. Dr. Perlmutter reports that Alzheimer's is present today in 5.4 million Americans and it is predicted that number will double by 2030! Even with our advanced brain scanning techniques, once one develops Alzheimer's, there is no known medical treatment whatsoever, and certainly no cure. Therefore early detection of this disease is moot. The only cure is prevention. The only prevention is dietary. Pharmaceuticals, generally speaking, are designed to treat symptoms and most have negative side effects. There are no magic pills to cure many common ailments that can be cured, reversed, and prevented with what you eat and don't eat.

I conclude this introduction with a quote from Johann Wolfgang von Goethe (1749-1832). I have taken this quote to heart for many years with great success in the execution of its content.

*Until one is committed, there is hesitancy, the*
*chance to draw back, always ineffectiveness.*
*Concerning all acts of initiative (and creation)*
*there is one elementary truth -- the ignorance of*
*which kills countless ideas and splendid plans:*
*That the moment one definitely commits oneself,*
*then Providence moves, too. All sorts of things*
*occur to help one that would never otherwise have*
*occurred. A whole stream of events issues from the*
*decision raising in one's favor all manner of*
*unforeseen incidents and meetings and material*

*assistance, which no man would have dreamed would*
*have come his way.*
*Whatever you can do, or dream you can do,*
*begin it.*
*Boldness has genius, power, and magic in it.*
*Begin it now.*

# CHAPTER

# MY PERSONAL TRANSITION

I began my journey from yo-yo fat to healthy slim in 2007 when I was first diagnosed with Mycological Syndrome (a systemic yeast/mold/fungal infection). Dr. Craig Reese, my primary care doctor, gave me a paper with printing on both sides. It is in alignment with Drs. Hyman and Perlmutter's dietary recommendations, but slightly more restrictive.

## THE YEAST DIET

Even though yeast won't give you a yeast infection, eating foods containing yeast and sugar in all forms, will aggravate the one you have. It is best to avoid foods that contain yeast, molds, sugar and fermented foods. <u>Examples</u> of these are:

AVOID

| | | |
|---|---|---|
| Sugar | Candy | Fruit Juice |
| Syrups | Fructose | Honey |
| Corn Syrup | Dried Fruits | Agave Nectar |
| Gluten | Chocolate | Cheese/cottage cheese |
| Mushrooms | Soy Sauce | Peanuts |
| Alcoholic Beverages | Artificial Sweeteners* | Bread w/yeast |
| Crackers w/yeast | Corn | Wheat |

*Except Stevia which is a sweet plant.

WHAT YOU CAN EAT

| | | |
|---|---|---|
| Meat & Fish | Vegetable Juice | Vinegar |
| Stevia | Vegetables | Water |
| Herbal Tea | Braggs Liquid Aminos | Brown Rice** |

**Brown rice in very small amounts (1/2 cup–1 cup/day)

The other side of the page informed me that Mycological Syndrome is another name for a combination of yeast, mold, and fungus infections. When the entire body is affected, they are referred to as being systemic. My symptoms were environmental and food allergies, asthma, anxiety, backaches, bloating, brain fog, chronic fatigue, constipation, digestive problems, headaches, joint pain, recurrent bacterial infections, colds, and flu.

The only time I was aware of this type infection was many years ago when I had a vaginal yeast infection where I cured the symptoms of it with the use of a topical over-the-counter drug, Monostat. However, Dr. Reese told me that whenever anyone has a vaginal yeast infection, they also have a systemic one.

He informed me that antibiotics, steroids, birth control pills, and parasitic infection cause Mycological Syndrome. I had taken all three prescription drugs at one time or another throughout my life. I had also been diagnosed with parasitic infections several times during the ten years prior to 2007.

If you would like to read his article on the subject, go to the internet site:

www.drcraigreese.com/InfoLetters/Yeast.html

## The website for his practice is:

www.drcraigreese.com

In 2007 I did not have a female yeast infection. I had a systemic one that was found after the blood work results were revealed. My symptoms were all of the previously mentioned.

I strictly adhered to the Yeast Diet and my weight came off effortlessly, even without a formal exercise program. Because I had more mental acuity, physical energy, and less pain than I had had in years, I assumed that the yeast was being healed by diet and pharmaceutical-grade food supplements alone. However, I was still using steroid nasal spray to control my Allergic Rhino and Asthmatic symptoms. Since the spray was topical it never occurred to me that it would harm me in any way. I did not realize that Allergic Rhino is Mycological Syndrome on the lining of sinus cavities. I did not share with Dr. Reese the fact that I was using steroid nasal spray twice a day, and had done so for the past twenty-four years. Unknowingly I was fueling the Mycological Syndrome in my sinus cavities in the worst way possible. I equate it with throwing gasoline onto an open fire. I was also unaware of any danger because the steroid nasal spray controlled the <u>symptoms</u> of Allergic Rhino and Asthma so completely.

I was feeling much better, losing weight, and went on for five years thinking I had been completely healed. I decided to commit to a lifestyle change with my new eating program as there were so many great benefits. I had no idea what a good decision that would be five years later.

In the autumn of 2011, I sought professional help to release past trauma from my body that was causing spontaneous panic attacks. Dr. Marilyn Adler referred me to an excellent trauma-release therapist, Dr. Pie Frey, both doctors located in Boulder, who used a technique called "Brain Spotting." This is a technique similar to Eye Movement Therapy (EMT). It was one of the most subtle, yet powerful, experiences of my life. This particular therapy gives all the control of the trauma-release process to the patient. After several sessions, I was literally heating up the room with the release of trauma my body had stored over the years.

February 23, 2012 during one session, <u>out of my eyes</u> popped red, itchy spots. They covered my eye lids, eye brows, forehead, and eventually my skull. The next day the red, itchy spots were diagnosed as Mycological Syndrome. My body had stored trauma which physiologically manifested as yeast! I later learned, energetically speaking, that yeast is all about emotions. I'll say! I now know that the daily use of steroid nasal spray for so many years was most likely the reason why the emotional trauma took on this physical form. I kept telling myself that because the nasal spray was topical, it was harmless. That ignorant lie cost me big time. Thus began one of the worst physically challenging ordeals of my life.

The location was bad enough, but the itch was indescribable. For the next thirteen months I almost lost my mind topically treating the itch caused by this infection. I came to learn that Mycological Syndrome has an intelligence of its own. In order to subdue the red, hot, and itchy symptoms, topical applications needed to be changed frequently because the infection becomes resistant to them all eventually.

Thirteen months after being treated internally and externally, I was infection free. In March 2013 several days after the itching stopped, my husband became very ill. Even though I had only three or four days free from the itch, I was grateful it stopped because I spent the next six months spending my waking hours caring for him; essentially living two lives at the same time. Thankfully he recovered to a point where he became mostly independent, but he still required our home to be installed with handicap accessories.

In the autumn of 2013 while I was having my yearly dermatological checkup, the doctor noticed I had a slightly red rash over my eyebrows.

He said it was Dermatitis. He gave me a sample prescription for a steroid cream and told me to use it for only three days and the rash would be healed. Unthinkingly and stupidly I used it for one application; then stopped because of a gut feeling. By December 2013 the Mycological Syndrome came back with a vengeance. My eyebrows (where I had applied the steroid cream) were hit worse than the first time in February 2012. By September 1, 2014 I still had waves of redness and itchiness, but they were mild and the infection was mostly gone.

There are times in all of our lives when we have regrets over the choices we make; those regrets come in the form of hindsight which is always 20/20. Other times when we look back on past choices, we are filled with gratitude and rejoice in them. This was a time when I couldn't have been more grateful for making the Yeast Diet a lifestyle change in 2007. Had I started eating products containing yeast and sugar (the substances which feed Mycological Syndrome) after I was healed the first time in 2007-2008, I can't imagine the horrible shape I would have been in five years later in 2012.

During my childhood and for the first fifty-five years of my life I was given frequent doses of antibiotics, usually to kill bacterial infections in both my sinus cavities and lungs. As a very young child I was given a penicillin injection (an antibiotic made from mold) almost every time my mother took me to the pediatrician. I had my first asthmatic attack at age five in 1952 when my allergy to cats revealed itself. I continued to develop allergies to everything in my outdoor environment throughout my childhood. At age sixteen, my pediatrician sent me to an allergy specialist. After being skin-tested, he prescribed allergy shots, three times a week for two years. They did little to improve my symptoms.

In 1967, at age twenty my ex-husband and I moved from Dallas, Texas to Boulder, Colorado. All my allergy and asthmatic symptoms disappeared. Many years later I discovered the reason for this was that I was mostly allergic to ragweed, pollen and dust mites which did not exist above 5,000 feet in altitude. I was divorced in 1975 and in 1979 when I moved to San Diego, California my allergies appeared once again. I was prescribed a steroid nasal spray so I could breathe more easily. I used it for a while but stopped.

Nine years later in 1988, my present husband and I were living in Los Angeles because of his job. I became very ill with a bacterial infection in my sinus cavities and lungs. Asthma became a problem as well. My doctor took a CAT-Scan of my head and told me I had a growth on the lining of my sinus cavities, but he didn't know what it was exactly. After he diagnosed me with Allergic Rhino (the growth) and Sinusitis (the bacterial infection), he explained that the Allergic Rhino creates a very moist environment which is a perfect one for bacterial infections to grow and thrive. It was not known then that the growth to which my doctor was referring was Mycological Syndrome. It was also not commonly known in 1988 that antibiotics and steroids are two of the root causes of this syndrome.

To control the allergic symptoms in my nose, he prescribed a steroid nasal spray. To kill the bacterial infection I was prescribed antibiotics. I was to irrigate with salt water five times a day, followed by an application of the nasal spray. It took me three years to be free from the recurring bacterial infection, Sinusitis. I went through every antibiotic on the market, becoming allergic to one brand, then switched to another. I can no longer take any brand of antibiotic without breaking out in red blisters all over my body. However, I still irrigate with salt water once, sometimes twice a day. I would recommend this practice to anyone. I use a Nasaline (syringe-type) adult nasal irrigator and the recommended Nasaline salt packets stirred into highly filtered water. Since I have been healed of this syndrome, the irrigation alone takes care of any nasal congestion I might have. I no longer have Asthma, Allergic Rhino, or Sinusitis since I have been healed of Mycological Syndrome, the root cause of those disorders.

What at first appeared to be an overwhelmingly, negative situation, eventually became a blessing in disguise. My life-long goal has been to have a slim and healthy body. To achieve this goal I went on one low-calorie, low-fat, diet after another only to become fat and sick. My lifelong goal was finally reached because I adhered to an eating regimen that was created to aid the healing of Mycological Syndrome. Hopefully this syndrome will not recur as I do not use steroids or antibiotics (topical or internal) to create future infections, and I do not eat sugar or yeast in any form to feed it.

Now that I am comfortable with my body size, energy level, and health, I live every day in gratitude. This way of eating has allowed me to break my addiction to sugar. I have no head hunger or cravings for any food. By eliminating sugar from my diet, I have reversed the onset of Type II Diabetes. I have as much energy and mental acuity as I had in my forties. Because of my body size, I no longer feel invisible to others in this society because of having an overweight body. I've learned the hard way that 'nothing tastes as good as being thin and healthy feels.'

# CHAPTER

# AMERICA'S OBESITY EPIDEMIC

## WHEN DID IT BEGIN?

If one observes the body sizes of people in movies and film clips taken during the first half of the 20th century, it quickly becomes obvious how thin the vast majority of Americans were before the 1950s. I was a child during that decade. I was not a fat baby. When I was in kindergarten until I reached the second grade in 1954, I was thin as was everyone around me including men, women, and other children. I would see an occasional over-weight person, but they were in the vast minority. When I asked my parents what made a person fat, the answer was either 'Diabetes' or 'Hereditary Glandular Disorder,' both of which were not the person's fault.

Today there is a rapidly spreading epidemic of obesity in this country, the likes of which has never been seen in human history. It affects women, men, and children alike. It is a phenomenon that crosses over all barriers including gender, race, culture, age, socio-economic class, and religion. Since we live in a culture which is, and has been for most of my life, obsessed with losing weight, why are so many Americans overweight? Theoretically, we should be a country filled with thin people.

During the first half of the 20th century listening to the radio was the center of American homes and family life. Pictures of that era depict families gathered together in their living rooms to listen to the radio. The children were usually sitting or lying on the floor, close to it. Women sat while doing some type of needle or yarn work. The men thumbed through a magazine or a newspaper. There was no food present in the room. No one was eating while listening to the radio. People spent their leisure time reading books, playing tennis, golfing, riding bicycles, playing table games, or participating in various other activities. Children played games with each other during their time away from school and homework. These games were not like the video or computer games children play today. They were board games like Monopoly and card games like Go Fish. Recreational activities and interaction with others were how people entertained themselves after a hard-day's work. There was no television to watch, no reason to eat anything after the completion of a meal, and the over-consumption of non-nutritive food was non-existent.

During those days, food was eaten for survival, not recreation. Cakes, pies, and desserts were served only on special occasions, not daily. They were made from scratch with non-GMO flour and cane sugar; not prepared in some factory, filled with High Fructose Corn Syrup (HFCS), preservatives, then packaged, and distributed. After those special-occasion dinners were finished, the dessert was served at the end of the meal and eaten at the dining room table. If ice cream was served at a picnic, it was usually homemade and created in a manual ice cream machine which required the laborious effort of cranking the handle for quite some time. There were ice cream parlors, cafes, and soda fountains where people went to eat ice cream and other sweet treats, but only occasionally; certainly not daily. Generally speaking, vanilla was the flavor and one scoop was the serving. Not only was the consumption of ice cream and other sweet foods an infrequent event, one had to take time and make an effort by leaving the home in order to obtain them. Candy bars as we know them today did not exist.

The Great Depression of the 1930s was a time during which people were literally starving in this country. Many could not afford to purchase any food, clothes, or the bare necessities. The lines in front of the soup kitchens were long and many people in those lines looked emaciated. Even those families who were not in those lines were still doing without many foodstuffs and other items. As a nation we had almost twelve years of real sacrifice as a run-up to World War II which began on December 7, 1941.

During the war, food was massively rationed in the then forty-eight United States. Foods rationed were sugar, bacon, butter, meat, tea, jam, biscuits, breakfast cereals, cheese, eggs, lard, milk, canned fruit, and dried fruit. Fresh vegetables and fruit were not rationed, but supplies were limited. Most foodstuffs were sent to our soldiers in Europe and the South Pacific who were fighting for our freedom and way of life. The Hershey bars that did exist, along with other non-perishable foodstuffs, were dropped by parachute over the countries we liberated. Our soldiers were given those same items to hand out to the starving survivors they encountered as the war ended. There were few, if any Hershey bars to be found here at home. I don't believe most people living in this country today truly understand the enormous sacrifice made by the generation of Americans who won the freedom some now take for granted. Every American citizen sacrificed in one way or another during World War II.

## HOW DID IT BEGIN?

By the time the war ended in August 1945 the vast majority of Americans had been through fifteen straight years of doing without many foodstuffs. Naturally, those who survived these years were ready to treat themselves to anything and everything once forbidden and now available. In 1951 when I was four years old, Hershey bars were not only plentiful, but affordable even to a child's weekly allowance. During the 1950s, candy manufacturers went into high-gear creating many different varieties of these new sweet treats, mass produced them, and widely distributed them. Every candy bar produced was sweetened with cane sugar; most were covered with chocolate. As soon as a new candy bar was available, it appeared in most grocery stores, gas stations, drug stores, and convenience stores.

At the same time, boxed cake mixes, packaged ready-to-eat cookies, a variety of canned goods, and other prepackaged fast foods were beginning to appear in grocery stores. Even though my mother was a full-time homemaker, she hated to cook. Anything prepackaged and ready to heat-and-serve was a godsend in her mind. Instead of having to wash, chop, and cook fresh vegetables, she was now able to open a can, heat the contents and serve them on a plate. Her favorite vegetables were canned green beans, which she boiled for thirty minutes before serving. The only salad I knew as a child was a square of some flavor Jello on top of an iceberg lettuce leaf, topped with a dollop of Miracle Whip. Many women who had worked outside the home during the war continued to do so after the war ended. They certainly had good reason to consider ready-to-eat food a needed time saver. Nutrition was not a widely studied subject. All varieties of food that once were rationed and now available were considered to be luxury items.

At the same time food became plentiful for all, televisions began to appear in homes around the country for the first time in history. Television of the early 1950s was a real novelty to the people who had survived the Great Depression and WWII. During that fifteen-year period of time, the only way to see a film or get news was to get dressed and go to a movie theater. Each film was followed by a newsreel which contained relatively old news. With the advent of this new modern marvel, Americans could be entertained and receive newscasts in the comfort of their homes. Television stations were being built and able to broadcast entertainment and more up-to-date newscasts now available with the touch of the T.V.'s 'on' switch.

Also during this time, post-war America became a mecca for the creation and mass production of large, electrical home appliances, not readily available or affordable before the war. The new, electric refrigerators with separate, big freezers were being delivered to the same homes where television sets were replacing radios as the center of family life. Ice cream and other prepared frozen products were appearing in grocery stores for the first time. The new electric freezers made these products available to all family members in their homes at an arm's reach. Store bought cookies and other ready-to-eat sweet foods began to appear on grocery store shelves making it unnecessary to expend the time and energy it took to bake cookies from scratch.

A perfect storm swept this nation into one of the biggest cultural changes in its history -- how Americans spent their leisure time. Inevitably, the combination of in-home, audio-visual entertainment and the convenience and abundance of sugary, high-carbohydrate, 'luxury' food began the era of recreational eating. Couch potatoes, by definition, became immobile as they ate junk food and watched TV during their leisure time substituting it for physical recreation. Most people who participated in this behavior eventually became overweight. Their children modeled this behavior, as did their grandchildren, and their great grandchildren. It is self-evident this was the beginning of the present-day obesity epidemic in America.

# THE YO-YO DIET CRAZE

The consensus of opinion in the 1950s was that food was food; a calorie was a calorie. A calorie of spinach was the same as a calorie of fruit cake. Food simply contained calories; some foods were higher in calories than others. If you ate more calories than you burned, you gained weight. If you ate fewer calories than you burned, you would lose weight. The only psychological component was that one must use willpower against any food craving. The highest caloric food is fat. One tablespoon of fat is 102 calories; 1 tablespoon of sugar is 17 calories. At age thirteen my mother put me on a 900-calorie-a-day diet. Since only calories counted, I found myself eating sandwiches made with white Wonder Bread, iceberg lettuce (least nutritional), Miracle Whip (less fat than mayonnaise), mustard, and bologna. I was allowed two store-bought cookies with a glass of skimmed milk after school. I was also allowed either ten jelly beans or ten gumdrops after dinner. She did this because she discovered a chart that listed what was considered to be an ideal weight according to sex and height. I weighed 125 pounds, but the chart said I should weigh 115 pounds. Thinking that she was acting in my best interest, she made it her mission to get ten pounds off of me. Although I did lose the weight, I felt hungry, weak, and craved something sweet to eat most of the time. I also craved butter and fatty meat.

At age sixteen my first boyfriend gave me a two-pound box of fancy chocolate candy for St. Valentine's Day. Since love was equated with sugar, I ate most of it and the ten pounds I originally lost were quickly back. It was at that point when I began obsessively craving sugary foods in general. When I was married at age eighteen I weighed 125 pounds. After being married to an abusive man for two years, I ate lots of sweet treats to numb the pain. Naturally my weight ballooned to 180 pounds. I felt trapped and helpless. This was in the late 1960s during a time when domestic violence was not as commonly known as it is today. Every time he drank alcohol when we were alone, I was abused. I thought I must have done something wrong to incur his wrath. I also thought I was the only woman in the world who was being abused. Since the abuse was mental, emotional and physical, I was ashamed and kept it a secret from everyone. My abuser had a charismatic personality to everyone else. Because the abuse occurred behind closed doors, no one would have believed me anyway. Naturally the pain of this abuse resulted in my having very low self-esteem. I needed to numb the emotional pain of this condition; my substance of abuse was sugar.

The first time I learned anything about nutrition was when I read and followed the original Weight Watchers diet when it came out in book form. After following the recommended eating regimen for several months, I did lose weight very slowly. I was supporting my ex-husband while he attended college by working in an office forty hours a week. It was a real struggle to follow the diet because of all the meal planning, grocery shopping, weighing, measuring, and food preparation. On the plus side I did get an education in basic nutrition.

Knowing then what I know now, I would have never chosen that eating strategy to lose weight. The daily diet allowed three servings of fruit, two pieces of bread, three servings of vegetables (some limited), ten ounces of lean protein and one tablespoon of fat. This was considered to be a well-balanced diet, the only healthy way in which to lose weight. That amount of sugar as fructose (in fruit) and complex carbohydrates (in bread) was keeping me head hungry and craving sugar all the time. In addition, the bread contained gluten. I did not know at that time I was a sugar addict with gluten sensitivity.

If I had tried to select the worst possible food for my body, I couldn't have done a better job!

With great time-consuming effort, I strictly adhered to the diet and eventually reached my goal weight of 125 pounds. I was still in my twenties and youth, in general, can overcome many obstacles that become more difficult with age. The real struggle was when my female hormones kicked in once a month, demanding that I consume chocolate, in any form, for at least three days.

Over time the domestic abuse escalated and I became obese. When my weight reached 182 pounds, I was desperate for any quick and easy weight-loss diet I could find. I tried the Grapefruit and Egg Diet, The Cabbage Soup Diet, The Banana Diet; the list goes on and on. They all allowed me to lose weight quickly, but I always felt deprived and craved sugar in any form. After enduring the deprivation of each extreme diet, I would tell myself I had earned and deserved 'just one' sweet treat. Once I took the first bite, I couldn't stop; I began binge-eating every sweet food in sight. If there was nothing sweet I could find at home, I drove to the store to get something.

This thinking pattern and the behavior it induces is the core of addiction. It took me decades to come to the realization that I was a hard-core sugar addict. Believing the lies I told myself to justify eating sugary foods and acting on those lies were the psychological and physiological reasons why I was obese. I even became addicted to weighing myself every morning. If I weighed more than the day before, I was in a bad mood; if I weighed less I was happy.

It never ended. Like a little animal running on a wheel inside a cage, the yo-yo diet phenomenon is an exercise in futility. No matter what new fad diet I found, and no matter how determined I was to stay on it, even if I reached my goal weight I never managed to maintain it for any length of time.

# THE FACE OF OBESITY IN AMERICA TODAY

I invite the reader to consider what substance is the real center of all American Holidays and celebrations. Beginning in February with chocolates on St. Valentine's Day, love is expressed with the giving and eating of chocolate. Usually within a month there is Easter which wouldn't be complete without chocolate bunnies and sugary Easter eggs. Birthdays, beginning with a baby's first, have cake and ice cream. What first birthday would be complete without a picture of a one-year-old child's cute little face and hands covered with cake and icing? Moving throughout the year, Memorial Day, July the 4th and Labor Day picnics have cold sweet treats like soda pops, ice cream treats, and snow cones. As the autumn months move into November, Halloween brings candy, candy, and more candy. Today's candy is sweetened with High Fructose Corn Syrup (HFCS) and is a very dangerous sweetener. Dr. Mark Hyman believes that sugar, especially in the form of HFCS, is more addictive than cocaine or heroin and is the single biggest killer in the 21st century. HFCS is contained in soft drinks, prepackaged, and fast foods consumed by Americans of all ages. For a full account of HFCS go to:

www.drhyman.com/blog/2011/05/13/5-reasons-high-fructose-corn-syrup-will-kill-you/#close

Less than a month after Halloween comes Thanksgiving, a holiday commonly associated with a turkey and all its trimmings as the center of the celebration. As a hard-core sugar addict, I used to gobble down (pardon the pun) the turkey and trimmings as fast as I could so I could get to all the various desserts. Pumpkin pie and pecan pie were my favorites. Within a week or two after Thanksgiving, the candy canes, sugar cookies, fudge, pies, cakes and desserts ring in the Christmas season which actually lasts until New Year's Day.

The scientific proof now shows that fat does not make you fat – sugar does. Sugar can be a powerfully addictive substance to some; it is an appetite stimulant to all. We've been told that fat makes us fat for the past sixty-five years. I remember it was during the 1980s fat-free era when I was first diagnosed with Hypoglycemia. This era ushered in prepackaged cookies, cupcakes, and sugary snacks which had fat removed from them and additional sugar added to them. Advertising cashed in on the fact that sugar was a better ingredient than fat because it was lower in calories, the accepted nutritional theory of the day. Dr. Mark Hyman estimates the average American today consumes 140 pounds of sugar per year! Until recently we have not been informed how powerfully negative the impact of sugar is on the human body. The distribution and widely accepted misinformation was not intentional, it was the only nutritional information available at the time.

If you want to understand the root of any problem, follow the money. The weight-loss diet industry is, and has been for decades, a very profitable venture. Look at all the professional weight loss centers that have opened their doors since the 1980s. Think of the large number of advertisements on television, magazines, and other publications promoting products and various ways in which to lose weight. At the same time the weight-loss ads appear, we are bombarded with high-sugar, junk food ads as well. Television and internet ads promote candy bars, sugary breakfast cereals, and fast food restaurants. These particular ads promise fast, delicious, and fun food. When did eating become fun? I think we all know when and where as these establishments are more plentiful today than when they were founded in the 1950s and 1960s. Fun implies eating to be a recreation. Most sugary products are aimed at children. How would you feel if you saw an ad aimed at children promoting heroin, cocaine, or alcohol? I remember the ad that finally awakened me when I was still addicted to nicotine. It was a T.V. ad which showed a fetus inside its mother's womb, smoking a cigarette. Advertisements are plentiful, appealing, and a very powerful way in which we receive information. I can remember jingles from early television commercials to this day. Never underestimate their impact on what you, your children, and loved ones eat!

## PERMANENT WEIGHT LOSS

Dr. Craig Reese's August 2014 newsletter gives information about permanent weight loss. He suggests that if you are eating a low fat and high grain diet and have gluten intolerance, weight loss, especially the loss of belly fat, will not be possible. If you are eating a high fat, low carbohydrate diet and eating cheese, the same holds true if you have an unknown lactose (dairy) intolerance. Any food allergy (known or unknown) can cause inflammation which causes internal swelling.

He suggests that we eat the way our grandmothers and great grandmothers ate. They grew their own organic vegetables or ate fresh vegetables from local farmers. No produce was picked unripe in a country far away and then shipped thousands of miles for consumption here in this country. All meat was free-range and grass fed. There were no farmed fish that were injected with food coloring to look like fresh fish.

Genetically Modified Organisms (GMOs) have altered our grains so much that native wheat is almost non-existent in this country. According to both Dr. Reese and Dr. Perlmutter, gluten intolerance is not a fad. Our bodies are mounting an attack against these foreign proteins (GMOs) because the human body is not programmed to process them. I have severe food allergies to both gluten and dairy. Not only did both these foods create inflammation in my joints, whenever I would eat a cheese sandwich, I had a sharp pain and severe gas for hours after eating it.

I spent five decades learning the hard way that low-calorie, heart-healthy diets for those like me with food allergies, sugar addiction, and gluten intolerance are total disasters. They all contain foods which appear on the Yeast Diet's AVOID list. In, Dr. Reese's newsletter of August 2014 he states: *"Larry Scott, the first Mr. America, Mr. Universe and Mr. Olympia said that 80% of body building (or just getting in shape) is nutrition."* I have never lost an ounce of weight with exercise alone. I have, however lost my excess weight and kept it off for years by staying active with housework and cooking fresh daily. It's a great thing if you are able and have the time to exercise, but it is what you eat that matters most.

In order to achieve permanent weight loss, one must first commit to a new lifestyle which removes the foods containing the ingredients that make a human body overweight and prone to health problems. Once the unhealthy foods are removed and the foods added which promote (1) weight loss, (2) maintenance of that loss, (3) reversal of blood sugar disorders, and (4) prevention and reversal of major health threats such as Diabetes and Alzheimer's, we will have won a big battle in the obesity epidemic. A country filled with people who are healthy, high energy, and motivated will naturally become a more economically prosperous nation. There will be no need to escape into any substance or behavior of abuse.

This is the dawn of a new era in nutrition and the scientific results are in:

FOODS TO REMOVE

- Sugar
- Carbohydrates
- Gluten

- Dairy if you have a sensitivity (which many people unknowingly do)

FOODS TO ADD

- Meat – Beef, Chicken, Pork
- Fish
- Dark colored and leafy vegetables
- Heart and brain healthy oils (e.g. avocado, walnut, almond, coconut, and olive)
- Real nuts (not peanuts)

In all forms, sugar is an appetite stimulant. The only sweetener that is acceptable is stevia because it is a plant and does not affect blood sugar levels. Complex carbohydrates (starches) are metabolized slower than sugar, but the body still processes them as sugar. For a complete scientific understanding about the impact sugar has on the human body, read the book *The Blood Sugar Solution* by Dr. Mark Hyman. His website is www.drhyman.com.

Breads made with wheat contain gluten. The human species did not have bread until the advent of agriculture 10,000 years ago; therefore our bodies are not programmed to digest it properly. Gluten creates systemic inflammation which creates swelling. Swelling in the brain leads to brain disorders. Swelling in the joints creates pain in them. Gluten also aggravates many other health problems, especially digestive ones. For a complete scientific understanding about the importance of removing gluten from your diet, I urge you to read the book *Grain Brain* or watch the PBS program *Brain Change* by Dr. David Perlmutter. His website is www.drperlmutter.com.

I have had the greatest success with Dr. Reese's Yeast Diet which is in alignment, but slightly more restrictive than the suggested eating regimens of Drs. Hyman and Perlmutter. I believe that is because I have (1) a life-long history and susceptibility to Mycological Syndrome; (2) Reactive Hypoglycemia and need to keep my blood sugar levels stable to prevent Diabetes; (3) multiple food allergies; and (4) gluten intolerance. The fewer carbohydrates (especially starches) I eat, the better I feel. Since I have been on the Yeast Diet my addiction to sugar has been eliminated.

# CHAPTER

# GETTING STARTED

## THE COMMITMENT

This way of eating is simple once you make the commitment and transition to it as outlined in this book. If you stay true to this eating strategy, you will lose all your excess weight with or without a formal exercise program. If I could walk thirty minutes or more a day, I would. You will also save time, money, and mental stress over your food consumption. Making the transition to this new plan can be daunting. The purpose of this detailed guide is to expedite this process while organizing your life at the same time. I was fortunate in that I already knew quite a bit about nutrition and had decades of experience with food preparation and cooking. I knew if I could prepare food that was delicious, satisfying, and have unlimited quantities of that food, I would be successful.

Past experiences with trying to lose weight on low-calorie diets dictate two big weaknesses: (1) the requirement to weigh and measure every ounce of food consumed, and (2) adhering to a complex list of rules. Consequently, I thought about food during most waking hours, naturally making me head hungry. Because those diets were high in sugar (fruit, bread, and other carbohydrates), my appetite was always stimulated. I believe most people who are trying to lose weight in that way detest the weighing and measuring aspect as well. It is self-evident that is why professional weight-loss centers came out with premeasured packaged food, easy to unwrap and eat, or heat and eat quickly. While those foods save time with initial weight loss, they contain sugar and unhealthy artificial sweeteners just like other prepackaged products. The only difference is that the portions are premeasured. Once you have reached your goal weight, the weighing-and-measuring-every-bite-you-eat begins once again as you attempt to maintain your goal weight.

Cooking fresh with organic vegetables, grass-fed beef, free-range chicken and cage-free eggs, real nuts, and healthy oil is the best way to nourish your body while the excess weight falls away. The time, energy, and stress are no longer a part of your life because there is no need to weigh or measure anything. With this new eating plan, eat as much of the foods on the plan as often as you like. Once you have done this for several weeks your body will be well nourished, which is the best appetite suppressant of all. Once sugar is completely removed from your daily intake, the sugar cravings and head hunger will stop. You will also begin to have better mental acuity and more energy. Simply focus on removing the foods under the AVOID section of the Yeast Diet and eat only the foods under the WHAT YOU CAN EAT section.

For those who can eat salads and raw vegetables, congratulations, but beware. If you choose to eat raw instead of cooked vegetables, I highly recommend you let them soak in an appropriate food cleanser for a while, then rinse thoroughly with filtered water to remove parasites and other contaminants before eating. Cooking vegetables is a much safer way to consume them. I cook all vegetables because my body is no longer able to digest raw food. All recipes for vegetables in this book are cooked in a wok. I do, however, have one salad dressing recipe that I use to pour over cold, cooked vegetables. It is found on Page 76.

Stevia is the only sugar substitute allowed. It is perhaps unique among food ingredients because it's most valued for what it doesn't do. It doesn't add calories nor does it affect the pancreas or blood sugar levels.

## THE PERMANENT SHOPPING LIST

The creation of a permanent shopping list is at the core of my success in meal planning, grocery shopping, food preparation, and storage. Not only does it organize, simplify, and save a lot of time every week, it also helps me to stay focused while at the grocery store. I stick to the list and don't even go down many aisles; this keeps me from purchasing things I don't need but might be tempted to put into my cart. The old adage is true: 'if you buy it, you wear it.'

I first created the concept of this type of list many years ago. My husband and I moved quite a bit the first ten years of our marriage because of his job. Just about the time I learned where the products were in a grocery store I patronized weekly, his job required us to relocate. Each time I went to a new grocery store for the first time, I carried a pad and pen with me. As I walked into the front door and came to the first section or aisle, I noted on the pad what items were there that I regularly purchase. Continuing through the store, I noted items I found at each aisle as I gathered them. When I was ready to check out I had the groceries I needed and a written compilation of where my items were located in the store listed in chronological order. Once home, I had all the information I needed to type a permanent grocery list I could use for future visits to that store. I made copies of the list and filed them away. The next time, and every time thereafter, until we moved again, I only needed to highlight the items I wanted on the list for future visits to that store. An example of one of my permanent shopping lists is on Page 26. I have a separate permanent shopping list for other stores where I purchase non-perishable items like paper products and cleaning supplies. The blank spaces are intentionally left for any special or seasonal items I can manually add before going to the store. This is an excellent tool for meal planning as it contains all the ingredients (or categories of food) you will be eating. The chronological order saves you time while shopping. From the time you enter the front door to the checkout, simply stick to the list. You will be amazed how quickly your shopping experience becomes.

The initial effort is naturally a bit time consuming; however it becomes worth every minute spent in the long run. The total amount of time it saves during future shopping trips is enormous. Using it anchors you to your commitment, saves you mental anguish over meal planning, and cuts the shopping experience in half because your mind is focused only on the foods you are purchasing when you are at the store. I believe this one page has organized a big part of my life and I can't imagine not having it.

# WHOLE FOODS

| | |
|---|---|
| AVOCADO/CHERRY TOMATOES | BASIL/OREGANO/TARRAGON |
| BROCCOLI | ONION POWDER/GARLIC POWDER |
| BABY BOK CHOY | CINNAMON |
| KALE | |
| CELERY | BULK RAW PECANS |
| CARROTS | RAW CASHEWS |
| CABBAGE | RAW ALMONDS |
| YELLOW SQUASH/ZUCHINNI | STEVIA, POWDERED |
| SPAGHETTI/WINTER SQUASH | BROWN RICE FLOUR |
| PEPPERS/RED/YELLOW/ORANGE | |
| LEMONS/ONIONS | BROWN MUSTARD STONE GROUD – EDEN BRAND |
| SPINACH/MIXED GREENS | MAYONNAISE |
| YAMS | |
| | CHICKEN BROTH |
| HAM THICK SLICE | TOMATO SAUCE |
| CHICKEN BREASTS/THIGHS | CANNED TOMATOES |
| PORK CHOPS | TOMATO PASTE |
| BONELESS PORK LOIN ROAST | |
| GROUND BEEF | ALMOND MILK |
| FILET MIGNON | |
| NEW YORK STEAK | FROZEN PEAS |
| PRIME RIB ROAST | PAPER PRODUCTS - STRAWS |
| BACON | PAPER PLATES |
| GROUND CHICKEN | |
| GROUND TURKEY | AUTO DW POWDER 7TH GENERATION |
| FROZEN LIVER | |
| FISH | TEA |
| | PAPER PLATES/STRAWS |
| EGGS | |
| EARTH BALANCE MARGERINE | FROZEN GLUTEN-FREE PRODUCTS |
| SOY FREE | |
| CELTIC GREY SEA SALT | |
| HAIN SEA SALT | |

# KITCHEN EQUPIMENT

The following list of small kitchen appliances and utensils will save time, be useful, and worth the expenditure if you don't already have them. Each item is considered to be a basic necessity because they streamline this food preparation process. I purchased all items listed below at Amazon.com. I found the highest quality for the price there.

- One or two <u>digital timers</u>. My all-time favorite is made by West Bend. It can count down which is the way I use it; however it also has the capacity to count up (like a stop watch). Electronic Timer, Cat. No. 40005X, Focus Electrics, LLC, West Bend, WI 53095 is available at a very reasonable price. I wouldn't think of preparing a meal without a timer. Setting timers for each step of a recipe or for each task performed around the home enables even a person over sixty or younger than sixteen to multi-task. It certainly prevents food from over-cooking; it is one of the best and least expensive time management tools I've ever found.
- <u>A stainless-steel wok with tight-fitting lid</u>. An electric, good quality one can be obtained for around $100. The Presto brand with a see-through lid is my favorite. A wooden stirring implement comes with the wok. Non-electric woks are less expensive, but not that much less when you consider how much you will use it. Do not purchase Teflon or non-stick woks. The high temperatures break down the coating quickly. They are a waste of money and not a healthy choice.
- A high-quality, stainless-steel, <u>12-inch skillet with a tight fitting, see-through lid</u>.

- <u>Large food processor</u>. If you don't have one, I suggest purchasing at least an 11-cup Cuisinart food processor; larger if you are cooking for more than four. I recommend this brand because I used the same Cuisinart food processor for more than thirty years and replaced it with another one several years ago.

- <u>High quality knives</u>. I am currently using J.A. Henckels brand of knives; the kind of knives which require sharpening. I wasted my money on serrated knives a couple of times and lived to regret it. Serrated ones do not require sharpening; they also do not last very long. With the amount of chopping and slicing you will do, the high-end, expensive knives are well worth the investment.

- <u>Knife sharpener</u>. I have never learned to use the long metal stick that some people use to sharpen their knives. I really like the Zwilling J.A. Henckels brand that sits on the countertop and has two openings so that each side of the blade is sharpened separately. It isn't expensive and is very easy to use. I sharpen each knife after each use.

- <u>Chopping Board</u>. To keep your knives sharper longer, purchase one made of polyethylene. I purchased a Prepworks from Progressive International PCB-1812 Cutting Board. It has a reservoir which collects liquids and controls the mess, an easy-grip handle, and is dishwasher safe.

- <u>Pyrex 2-cup measuring cup with a handle and pouring spout</u>. These are available at most grocery stores.

- <u>Pyrex rectangular storage containers with plastic tops</u>. During the week I use six of the 11-cup capacity containers; in addition I use two of the very small and two of the medium sized rectangular storage containers as well. Glass is the best material in which to store left over food; Pyrex is heavy duty and can be used to cook in the microwave, regular oven, and store leftovers in the freezer.

- <u>Stainless steel implements</u>: spatula, large slotted spoon, large solid serving spoon, and tongs.
- <u>A meat thermometer.</u>
- <u>Large serving bowls, salad bowls</u> to hold the chopped vegetables before placing into the wok. I fill two bowls for one wok cooking.
- <u>An electric mixer.</u> I have a Kitchen Aid brand mix master with a large bowl. I use both a food processor and mix master. However, if I had to choose between the two I would choose a food processor.
- <u>Stainless steel, 6 quart Stewpot with Colander and lid.</u>

# CHAPTER

# FOOD FOR THOUGHT

## CREATE NEW ENVIRONMENTS

Set yourself up for success. If you are committing to this new way of eating, the top of your priority list needs to be the removal of all stored foods listed under the AVOID section of the Yeast Diet. This is particularly important if you are addicted to sugar. You need to safe-proof your kitchen shelves, pantry, refrigerator, freezer, purse, car, work place, or any other environment you inhabit. This is similar to baby-proofing cabinets which contain toxic, cleaning products. If you want to remove sugar from your diet, you first need to remove it from where you live. Keep in mind that once you have collected the new food items from the grocery store, you can eat unlimited quantities of them. Your body will quickly become smaller and your energy level and mental acuity will greatly increase.

I remember the mental struggle I had when I began to throw away an expensive bag of fructose and some jars of fruit I had just purchased. The thoughts that went through my mind were: 'I hate to waste food and money, so I'll save it, set it aside and take it to a food bank.' or 'I know my friend Sally really likes to bake; so I'll save that bag of chocolate chips to take with me and give it to her the next time we get together.' Any amount of time that passes between your commitment to remove sugar from your life and the actual removal of it is too long. Once you have removed those old items from your shelves, throw them in the trash can and take it to the curb! This is what live-in rehabilitation centers do for their clients. Keep in mind that you are not wasting money; instead you are ridding your life of addictive poisons.

If you are addicted to sugar, whenever you are reminded of a food with sugar in it, mentally re-define it as not edible. Now when I look at a sugary food, my brain registers it as being a plastic object. The old 1950s idea of just using willpower when it comes to addiction is ridiculous. People who suffer with addiction may have discipline in other areas of their lives, but when it comes to their substance (or behavior) of abuse, simply using self-control is completely ineffective.

If my tone seems extreme, perhaps it is because I have lived through and conquered this addiction just as I did decades ago with nicotine. My addiction to sugar made me abuse it over a sixty-year period which left me obese and very ill. There is no doubt in my mind that had I continued to eat it, I would have insulin-dependent Type II Diabetes today. Thankfully, I stopped just in the nick of time.

## BEHAVIORAL TIPS

Back in the 1970s I saw a poster that read: 'You're not what you think you are, but what you think, you are.' Another adage of that same era is: 'Whatever the mind can conceive and believe it can also achieve.' The book, *The Inner Game of Tennis* and other books of the time were in alignment with the above aphorisms; all conveying the importance of a person's thoughts. Naturally, a positive attitude will enable a more productive and rewarding life. However, even with a positive attitude addiction is a very complex problem that requires mental work as well as physical effort, one day at a time. When I tried to quit smoking numerous times before I finally became a non-smoker, I had a positive attitude. I still needed to create specific

31

behaviors I could use to aid in the elimination of that addiction. When I made the commitment to remove sugar from my life, many of the same behaviors I used to become a non-smoker translated successfully. Addiction is addiction; only the substance of abuse changes. Once I stayed on the Yeast Diet for several weeks, the sugar cravings were greatly lessened; after a while they were completely gone.

Once you have successfully made the transition from the foods which made you overweight and sick to the foods that will make you permanently slim, you will still need to carry on with daily living. The following tips are to help you live your life as you choose without straying from your new lifestyle commitment.

- GROCERY SHOPPING LIST. Never go grocery shopping on an empty stomach or without a list. Always stick to the list. This will save you time and money, and prevent you from purchasing something that is not on your new eating strategy. A sample of a permanent grocery shopping list is on Page 26.
- MENTALLY RE-DEFINE THE WORD TREAT. When I was addicted to sugar, to me the only definition of the word treat was something sweet to eat. The Merriam-Webster Dictionary defines treat as 'to provide with enjoyment or gratification.' There are many non-edible ways in which to enjoy life without eating junk food. Think of things you enjoy doing that have no association with food. Since the best appetite suppressant is a well-nourished body, staying on this eating regimen will certainly give you one. Give yourself ten days to three weeks without any sugar and you will lose the cravings and head hunger.

- ASSOCIATIONS AND TRIGGERS. When I was addicted to sugar, there were numerous external reminders of how delicious sugary foods taste. The smell of baked goods, advertisements with pictures of candy or cake, and people talking about how delicious a certain dessert tastes, are just a few examples of what can trigger a sugar craving. Once you stop eating sugary foods, you will probably find yourself bombarded with all sorts of situations which can make you want to eat something sweet. This is why it so very important to start working on your beliefs about sugar as a non-edible substance instead of a treat. When these triggers occur, take a moment to stop and change your mental definition of a sugary food from that of a delightful treat to that of something non-edible.

- SOCIAL FUNCTIONS. Before you leave to go to a party or any social gathering, eat a full meal. Take a bottle of filtered water with you in case there is no club soda or bottled water available at the function. Try to stay as far away from the food table as possible until you reach the point where your food cravings are not triggered by the sight and smell of party food. Instead of eating while mingling through the crowd, make your purpose for being there one of socializing with the other guests. Without trying to juggle a plate of food and a drink as you converse with others, you will be less physically encumbered.

- DELAYED GRATIFICATION. This is a psychological trick I learned many years ago when I quit smoking. If you have forgotten to stock your purse or car with your new food and have a head-hunger craving, tell yourself that you will satisfy it, but just not right now. Think of the delicious food waiting for you at home that you can eat as soon as you walk in the door. This is one reason why it is so very important to always have your new food in the refrigerator, ready to eat or microwave and eat. For example, you might be out shopping and your internal fast-food voice is insisting that you stop and get something to eat right this minute! The delayed gratification thought replaces the I-need-to-eat-right-this-minute one. Make it a habit to always have some healthy food with you. I carry turkey sticks, nuts, beef jerky or some form of protein in my purse.

- FAMILY AND FRIENDS. It has been my experience that even those people who are supposed to love you the most, and be supportive of you in every way, can become uncomfortable with the new, thinner you. It is possible that they will unconsciously sabotage you with various covertly negative comments. Some people are simply trying to process the fact that you no longer eat sugar in any form. It is human nature for some people to be jealous of success. Your success might remind them of what they are trying hard to ignore within themselves. Perhaps they are overweight and are afraid they might me expected to stop eating sugar too. They might be addicted to sugar but are afraid to acknowledge that fact to themselves and others. No one enjoys feeling guilty about anything. The comments may sound something like: 'just one piece of cake doesn't hurt anyone' or 'why can't you try just one bite; after all, I spent hours baking this pie.' It goes on and on and I'm certain the reader who has been a victim of the yo-yo-diet syndrome can relate to this phenomenon. Ask yourself, would anyone force a recovering alcoholic to drink 'just one' alcoholic beverage? As the late Robin Williams stated in an interview about addiction, the little voice in your head saying 'just one' is the voice of addiction.

- JUST SAY I DON'T. When I quit smoking cigarettes many years ago, I found that there was personal power by using the phrase 'I don't smoke' instead of 'I quit smoking.' The difference might seem trite, but it is powerful. 'I don't' is an absolute; 'I quit' implies the possibility of starting again in the future. The same is true with sugar, party food, fast food, and any food not on your new eating plan. When I say 'I don't eat sugar,' people usually ask me what I do eat. I tell them I only eat protein, vegetables, and real nuts. Most are taken aback and shocked at first. This is a natural and understandable reaction until they have processed the concept of my choosing a whole new lifestyle. If anyone starts pressuring me with questions, I state: 'since my blood work indicates that I am heading toward insulin-dependent Diabetes, I am choosing to prevent the onset of it with diet.' Once the word Diabetes is mentioned, most people get the message. If someone gives you a really hard time and continues to pressure you into eating something not on your new eating regimen, you might want to ask yourself if they are a true friend. If you stay strong and true to your commitment, lose weight, look smaller, and exude high energy, you will set an example for others who might be inspired to do the same for themselves. Anyone who continues to try to sabotage your commitment after you have thoroughly explained the situation to them is energetically toxic to you.

- FEED YOURSELF MENTALLY. At least in the beginning, turn off the television when you eat a meal. Listening to music is a better choice if you need external input while you are refueling. Pay full attention to the food you are eating. Close your eyes, taste and savor each bite. To aid in this endeavor, put your fork or spoon down between bites. There is a fifteen- to twenty-minute time delay from the moment you put food in your mouth to the time when your brain registers that your stomach is being filled. Eating slowly and deliberately are excellent behaviors to choose. With no television to watch while eating food at the same time, a perfect opportunity presents itself to begin breaking the habit of recreational eating.

- RECREATIONAL EATING. When you change the way you think of food from living to eat to eating to live, then you will be able to stop eating recreationally. This is a multi-generational behavior that began with the advent of television and prepackaged, ready-to-eat junk food readily available in our homes since the early 1950s. How is that working for us? If you are eating while watching television at the same time, you are eating unconsciously, almost in a trance-like state. Your attention is on the television, not on the food you are eating. Because recreational eating is so engrained in our culture, if you need to watch television while eating, make sure it's food from the WHAT YOU CAN EAT section of your new food plan.

- EMOTIONAL EATING. Some people eat when they are sad; others eat when they are happy or want to celebrate. I could justify eating sugary foods for any reason. I have often heard it said that people stuff themselves to cover emotional pain. I certainly did. People eat during highly stressful times in their lives. Who isn't stressed these days? I have Post Traumatic Stress Disorder (PTSD); stress and anxiety have been at my core for decades. At age eighteen I was diagnosed with my first panic attack; then known as shell shock. I justified eating sugary foods while I was emotionally upset which simply led to a sick and overweight body. While my mind could justify this behavior, my body didn't get the memo! The body simply processes junk food by storing it as fat. Unlike the mind, the body does its job without emotion or reason.

- GRAZE EATING. Like cows and horses eat grass in their respective pastures, some people 'graze eat' junk food during all waking hours. I believe all types of eating behaviors which add unwanted pounds to the body, contain sugar in some form. Since it is an appetite stimulant, head hunger is present all the time. While it is easier on the digestive system to have more, smaller meals instead of two or three big meals, make sure to eat only those food allowed on your new eating program.

- SUGAR ADDICTION. Sugar is a tough addiction to break. This substance is socially acceptable and prevalent throughout the American culture. Soft drinks alone are consumed by people of all ages. Did you know that artificial sweeteners (other than Stevia) affect the human body in as negative a way, if not more so, than sugar? On his T.V. show Dr. Frank Oz has shown that artificial sweeteners are more fattening than sugar because of the way the human body processes them. I believe that sugar will be to the 21$^{st}$ century as nicotine was to the 20$^{th}$ century. Sugar is much more socially acceptable and prevalent throughout the American culture than nicotine ever was. People start eating it at a much younger age than anyone started smoking. And, last but not least, sugar is equated with love.

- SUGAR EQUATED AND ASSOCIATED WITH LOVE. Be aware of this phenomenon in our society. I can remember throughout my childhood, every time I hurt myself, my mother would 'make it better' by giving me cookies and milk. The baking and giving of sugary foods is traditional and a widely accepted way to show love in our society.

- STAY HYDRATED. Whatever you need to do to keep filtered drinking water at an arm's reach throughout the day, do it. Keep bottled drinking water in your car, in your purse/backpack, on your desk at work, and close at hand during all waking hours. You need a minimum of ten, 8-ounce-glasses of water every day. This amount of water is in addition to the consumption of other liquids. Drinking plenty of filtered drinking water is one of the healthiest things you can do for your body. It also helps curb your appetite.

- PROGRAM YOUR MIND FOR SUCCESS. Monitor your thoughts. Take time throughout the day to stop what you are doing and pay attention to what you are thinking. If you find yourself thinking of sugary foods and have feelings of sacrifice and deprivation, replace them with thoughts such as 'I can eat any time I get hungry in unlimited quantities of my new foods.' If you are having real difficulty with sugar cravings, eat more protein. Remember, you can eat any time you get hungry and eat as much as you want. This type of thinking removes the fear of deprivation.

- LEISURE TIME. It is important to treat yourself by doing things you enjoy that do not require food. If you already have a hobby like knitting, reading, artwork, or something that occupies your leisure time, you are ahead of the game. If you are able, take a walk outside, explore a subject of interest on the internet, or take up a hobby. Pamper yourself with a warm soak in the bathtub; light some candles and listen to some relaxing music. If at all possible, schedule regular massages into your life. Learn to meditate and do so whenever you have the opportunity. Meditation is simply finding a quiet place in which to clear your mind of all thoughts. Breathe deeply and relax. Meditation takes practice, but has many benefits. Most importantly, give yourself some quiet time daily in the third dimension. Everyone today seems to be preoccupied with cyber space. Humans are intrinsically spiritual by nature. We need to be fully present in the third dimension without external input for some time each day. Our bodies need this time as much as they need air, water, food, and sleep. It is during this time in which we have the opportunity to observe our thoughts and fine tune them for success.

## THE INNER KEY TO SUCCESS

Live with an attitude of gratitude and abundance instead of deprivation and want. No matter how negative or stressful your situation might be, remember it can always be worse. A negative attitude of self-pity is as much a saboteur to your success as consuming sugar. Instead of thinking about all the foods you miss, think about the unlimited quantities and varieties of the new foods you have chosen that will make you thin, feel younger, and give you more energy. Let your creativity flourish by thinking of new flavors you can add to vegetables, meat, and nuts when you prepare them.

Make a genuine commitment to yourself and stick with it, one day at a time. If you shift your focus to eating only the foods allowed on this new plan, the weight will come off as a side effect. The changes you will need to make in order to achieve a thin and healthy body have been listed previously. They are specific suggestions you can take that will make your transition easy and short in duration. Remember yourself. Whenever you find your thoughts straying from this commitment, ask yourself: 'Am I contemplating eating a food not on my new food plan because I want to fit in with others around me?' 'Why am I even thinking about eating something I have chosen to not eat?' Peer pressure can be very strong. When it comes to what you put in your mouth, you and only you are the one in control.

If you are a stay-at-home mother or father raising children, now is the time to teach your children life-long lessons in good nutrition by example. Start teaching them how to cook healthy food early in life. If you are allowing your children to eat only high sugar, high carbohydrate, junk, and fast food, you are dooming them to a life of obesity and disease. You are the adult. You are the one who purchases, cooks, and serves your family's meals. If your spouse or children complain about this new way of eating, don't give them a vote. And don't enable them by cooking a separate meal! They have many opportunities to eat junk food throughout every day, but you don't have to be the one who serves it to them.

Teach your children to prepare and cook fresh foods. This is a skill every person who eats needs to know. If you aren't already teaching your children how to cook, do so now as these are their best learning years. If you want them to grow up to become independent and healthy adults, teach them these basic skills now. Cooking requires discipline and planning; two concepts that some would say are almost extinct in young people. Learning self-discipline as a child will enable them to achieve at a higher level in all areas as they grow into adults. Learning basic cooking skills will give them an advantage throughout the rest of their lives.

Since this country equates sugar with love and celebration, the connection between the two is so strong that it is even an integral part of our vernacular. (e.g., she is such a sweet person; let me call you sweetheart, nicknames like honey, sugar, and sweetie pie, etc.) American society is saturated with sugar in every form imaginable – edible and otherwise. By necessity sugar became a 'forbidden fruit', literally and psychologically, during the Great Depression and World War II. Once sugar became readily available in a multitude of forms in our homes and other environments, the over-consumption of it and addiction to it has become prevalent throughout our society. Many of us have paid the price by living in overweight, low-energy, sickly, and often painful bodies.

The over consumption of sugar is the main cause of Type II Diabetes. The treatment of this disease is big business. At best it requires monitoring equipment to test blood sugar levels throughout the day and daily insulin injections; at worst it necessitates the amputation of a limb and/or losing one's eyesight. Because this disease has become so widespread throughout American culture, Diabetes is becoming socially acceptable. This is a perfect example of how powerful an addiction sugar really is. I'll never forget a conversation I had with an old friend with whom I was raised. When I asked her if she was concerned about contracting Diabetes because of all the sugar contained in her diet, she said: 'oh, everyone I know has just a little bit of Diabetes.'

Amputation is a subject no one wants to think about. However, there are moments in everyone's life that startle and awaken. When my mother was in the hospital shortly before she passed away, she was sharing a room with a morbidly obese woman who had to have her foot amputated because of Diabetic complications. I saw her the day before the surgery and the day after. The day before she was assuring

41

all her family and loved ones that while she was a bit anxious over the surgery itself, she was confident the procedure would solve all her problems. The day after the surgery, she was screaming in agony that she could still feel her foot even though her foot was gone. Ask yourself 'does any sweet food taste good enough to risk losing a limb?'

You and only you put food in your mouth. This book shows you the simplest, easiest, and healthiest way to obtain and maintain a slim and healthy body. While it is 'the road less traveled,' I invite you to take the journey. The rewards are so great it is impossible to put them into words. I cannot think of any other commitment I've made to myself that has garnered so many unimaginable rewards.

# CHAPTER

# FOOD PREPARATION

## IN GENERAL

Since I like to cook, eat delicious food, clean up, and get out of the kitchen as quickly as possible, most of the meat recipes are cooked in a 12-inch, stainless steel skillet with a tight-fitting see-through lid. I prepare filet mignon and pork roasts by browning them in a skillet, then place them in the oven for final cooking. All the vegetable recipes are cooked in an electric, stainless steel wok. Although there are only two of us, I prepare both meat and vegetables in portions that will feed four. This cuts cooking time in half because it automatically gives me two meals instead of one.

Leftovers are the ingredients for some fast, sometimes cold, meals. Having leftovers in the refrigerator, ready to eat or heat-and-eat, is the core of success on this lifestyle program. Weekly I use six 11-cup rectangular Pyrex storage containers with heavy plastic lids. In addition I use two very small and two medium sized, rectangular Pyrex dishes with lids. They are all used for storage in the refrigerator after the initial dish is cooked. The same Pyrex dish containing leftovers is covered with Cling Wrap and heated in the microwave when another meal is needed. These particular storage containers stack easily and efficiently because of their shape. Pyrex or glass is the best material for food storage. Storing cooked vegetables separately from meat dishes has the following benefits:

- Previously cooked, cold chicken (or other meat) can be turned into a cold meat salad by either chopping it into bite sized pieces or placing small chunks into a food processor with the knife blade. Hit the 'process' key. Mayonnaise or some other type of oil (avocado, almond, or walnut) may be required to achieve the desired texture of the final recipe. Once blended, it can be placed on top of a sliced avocado or other vegetables you like. This is fast and easy because, if you use my vinegar, stevia, salt and water method shown below, the meat rarely requires any additional flavor added to it. Often it doesn't even require adding mayonnaise because there is olive oil still in the dish from when it was cooked.

- Previously cooked vegetables stay fresher longer in the refrigerator than raw ones do.

- Storing meat separately from vegetables gives you more options when leftovers are combined to create new meals. Since leftovers can be served hot or cold, even more options are available when you store the meat and vegetables separately. This is analogous to extending your wardrobe by purchasing compatible tops and bottoms.

- Most cooked dishes taste better after they have stayed in the refrigerator overnight or longer.

I have been preparing meals for more than fifty years so I don't depend on exact measurements that come with the recipes found in magazines, cookbooks, and the internet as some cooks need to do. When I began to change my approach to food more than seven years ago, I could not find recipes that contained only the foods I needed to eat. It was necessary for me to either create the recipes with my imagination and experience, or find an already-printed recipe that

I could alter by substituting my new food with the food contained in the printed one. I measure by sight, taste-as-I-go, and remember past cooking successes and failures. Therefore, most recipes in this book are more in the form of a 'method of cooking' rather than exact measurements. I use the symbol ~ which represents the word approximately. Everyone's taste is different so I encourage you to add or subtract from these approximate amounts according to your taste. In general, the old adage 'less is more' is a good way to approach the preparation of any recipe. It is naturally easier to add than subtract when getting the flavor you want. This applies especially to the use of salt, vinegar and stevia. I use all three ingredients in both meat and vegetable dishes.

If you are looking for cookbooks that will follow the food plan I follow, I can recommend *The Blood Sugar Solution Cookbook* by Dr. Mark Hyman, and *The Grain Brain Cookbook* by Dr. David Perlmutter.

## SUBSTITUTION OF INGREDIENTS

One simple way to make Italian meatballs or meat loaf gluten free is to substitute brown rice flour for the bread crumbs. Cook some spaghetti squash in the microwave and you now have gluten and starch free noodles. See MEATBALLS & SPAGHETTI on Page 69.

Since I love mashed potatoes, but white ones are high in sugar, I used well-cooked, well-drained, cauliflower instead. See CAULIFLOWER MASHED POTATOES on Page 53. This is an original Weight Watchers recipe that has been around for decades. If you cook a creamy chicken recipe, the gravy can be poured over the cauliflower just as you would over mashed potatoes. By learning how to substitute, you can eat your new foods without feeling deprived.

While perusing through most pre-printed recipes I am struck by the fact that we are a nation of cheese eaters. I have not found a substitute for cheese in recipes. Since I am lactose intolerant, I cannot eat any dairy. If you have Mycological Syndrome, cheese is on the AVOID section of the Yeast Diet. Cheese, especially in the large quantity Americans eat it, is not necessarily a high-protein choice. Cheese contains 26 percent protein and 72 percent saturated fat. Lactose intolerant or not, the body produces mucus with the consumption of dairy products. With the amount of present day air pollution, isn't it difficult enough to breathe without it? When you think about it, nature provides cow's milk for one purpose: to feed calves until they are old enough to eat on their own. Less than one-hundred years ago, cows were all free-range, eating grass without pesticides, were not injected with hormones and antibiotics, and not eating GMO grain. The animals themselves were eating cleaner. That was then, and this is now. Only you can decide whether your body can tolerate dairy products. If you have an unknown food allergy or sensitivity to dairy, it will be almost impossible to lose your belly fat. Any food sensitivity can create inflammation and swelling in your body.

While I have not been successful in finding a substitution for cheese, when a recipe calls for milk I use unsweetened, Blue Diamond Almond Milk. If it needs a bit of sweetness I add very small amount of powdered Stevia.

Eating gluten free has become much easier today than ever before. However, just because a product is labeled gluten free does not mean it is a good choice. Most prepackaged products which are gluten free are also full of carbohydrates and sugar. Brown rice is intrinsically gluten free; and only one-half to one cup of cooked brown rice is permitted per day. I no longer eat brown rice. Instead, I use Brown Rice Flour in cooking chicken breasts and other meats.

## VEGETABLES

When I prepare and cook both the vegetables and meat recipes for the same meal, I cook them separately. The vegetables are cooked in an electric wok; the meat recipes are cooked in a stainless-steel skillet with a tight-fitting lid. First the vegetables are prepared and cooked as their preparation time is usually longer than the meat dishes cooked in the skillet. The vegetables require washing and chopping before they are cooked. Onions do not need washing because their thick skins are cut away and discarded before chopping them. Choosing two or three different colored vegetables makes the final dish more visually appealing. Chopping all vegetables to be about the same size ensures they will cook evenly. An electric wok is at the center of my kitchen, but woks also are available to set on top of your stovetop. A wok is the perfect size and shape for cooking all the vegetables now required for your new eating strategy.

ONIONS are very flavorful and I add them to most vegetable dishes. Purple (red) Onions are my favorite. After the wok is heated, I put the onions in first, stir, and let them cook 45 seconds to flavor the oil before adding the other vegetables.

GARLIC is also a very flavorful ingredient. If you are using crushed or chopped garlic from a jar, be very careful because of the water content. Turn the wok on warm or very low. Add the oil and immediately add a Tablespoon or two of the garlic into the warm oil and stir continuously for about 30 seconds. After the garlic is beginning to cook, add the remaining chopped vegetables and raise the temperature to 300°F; completely mix the vegetables in the wok so all vegetables are covered with oil and garlic. Pour the heated and completely combined flavor mixture (vinegar, stevia, salt, and water) over the vegetables. Cover with the wok's lid and turn the temperature up to highest setting only until the liquid boils. Then turn down to 250°-300°F with the lid on to complete cooking.

KALE (also known as the healthiest green vegetable) is bland, slightly bitter in taste with a very dense fiber. Therefore, it requires some real zip added for its flavor and needs to be cooked for a lot longer than most vegetables. See SWEET AND SOUR KALE on Page 54.

Kale, carrots, celery, and purple onion make a nice colored vegetable mix. The kale, carrots, and celery take the longest cooking time of all vegetables listed, so cooking them together makes a nice mix.

BROCCOLI – follow the flavor directions above for Kale, just don't cook quite as long. Test with a fork as they are cooking.

SPINACH (another very healthy choice) is bland, but not as dense in fiber as kale. Actually spinach's fiber is the opposite of dense and takes a short time to cook. Garlic and/or onion add flavor. A recipe for cooking spinach in a wok in on Page 56.

CARROTS (another dark colored vegetable) take as long a time to cook as kale. I purchase the little ones in the bags that are ready to use. If you want to prepare only carrots, heat the wok on 200°F for 30 seconds, add oil and sprinkle with either cinnamon, curry, or your favorite spice. This pre-seasons the oil. Then add the carrots and stir for a minute until the carrots are completely coated in the seasoned oil. For the liquid I suggest a small amount of light-vinegar, small amount of Stevia (optional), small amount of salt, then water. If you like fully cooked, you might need to add more water as they cook down.

ZUCCHINI/YELLOW NECK SQUASH (are good in mixed vegetable dishes). Instead of flavoring zucchini, sometime I use tomato sauce instead of vinegar. The tomato sauce requires less Stevia because it doesn't have the "bite" that vinegar does. Basil, Parsley, Oregano, and granulated Garlic Powder will give them an Italian flavor. See ZUCCHINI ITALIAN STYLE on Page 58.

RED/YELLOW/ORANGE BELL PEPPERS are colorful ways to add to other vegetables for a more eye-appealing presentation. The most important thing to remember about the preparation of these peppers is to make certain all the seeds are removed before final chopping.

BOK CHOY is a vegetable that requires about the same intensity of flavors and cooking time as zucchini or yellow neck squash.

FROZEN ORGANIC SWEET PEAS are a quick and easy vegetable choice for a meal. Do not overcook frozen peas! The best texture and flavor is achieved by placing them in a sauce pan with some water. Bring to just boiling, then remove from heat and let rest for several minutes.

## BASIC STEPS FOR WOK COOKING

The following are some basic steps, in chronological order, to streamline cooking vegetables in the wok. Once you use this cooking method, you will quickly understand why a wok is necessary. The daily consumption of vegetables is voluminous and a wok is designed for that purpose. An electric wok comes with a wooden paddle for stirring and a tight-fitting lid. The lid allows for steaming, which is the method I use. I have never used the Chinese method of high-temperature, wok cooking. The only time I turn the wok's dial to its highest temperature is right after I add the liquid in order to speed the boiling process. After it begins to boil I turn it back down to about 300°F.

Always pre-heat the wok before adding oil; this will prevent the oil from smoking or burning.

Before you plug in or pre-heat the wok, follow the basic steps listed below:

- In a 2-cup Pyrex pouring cup with a handle, place 1-2 Tablespoons vinegar (fig, peach or golden balsamic are my favorites) into the bottom; then add powered stevia (~2 teaspoons) on top of the vinegar; add 1 Tablespoon of Light Grey Celtic sea salt.
- Fill the rest of the cup with water and stir. Taste to see if you need to add more of some ingredient. If you get too much of one, add water to dilute.
- Place into microwave. Heat on high for about 2 minutes. This makes the combination of all ingredients easier.
- Stir completely and set beside the wok.
- Get out bottle of Olive Oil, remove the top, and place it beside the cold, unplugged wok.
- Wash, rinse, pat dry, and place vegetables on chopping board. Chop vegetables into bite sizes. Use enough raw vegetables to fill two large serving bowls
- Place the bowls of chopped vegetables beside the wok.
- If garlic is not in the recipe, turn the wok to 250° - 350°F. Within 30 seconds, hold your hand about six inches over

the bottom to feel it is becoming hot. It will start to heat immediately.

- As soon as you can feel the heat, pour the oil into the bottom of the wok.
- For most recipes, place all the vegetables at one time into the wok. There are some recipes which require vegetables to be added separately, but that is rare.
- Stir vegetables until they are all covered with oil and begin to cook.
- Pour the contents contained in the 2-cup Pyrex pouring cup over the vegetables. Add one additional cup of water and stir vegetables completely.
- Place the lid on the wok.
- Turn the wok's dial up to the highest setting until the liquid begins to boil. Once it does, turn it down to about 300°F and cook until a fork can easily pierce the vegetables. The time you cook it depends on whether you like them "al-dente" or fully cooked. Fully cooked takes about 20-25 minutes, depending on the type of vegetables you are cooking. This amount of vegetables yields 4-6 servings.
- Periodically lift lid and stir the vegetables until they are cooked to the texture you want.

Once the vegetables are cooked, you can remove them from the wok easily with a large, slotted spoon.

Cooking any fresh vegetable can be quick, easy and delicious by following the above-mentioned BASIC STEPS FOR WOK COOKING. The flavor of the vegetables depends on the liquid poured over them while they are cooking.

## THE FLAVOR FACTOR

People who have been cooking a while realize that the actual flavor is not necessarily found in the basic food. Chicken, fish, and other meats are rather bland if not seasoned properly. One must add at least salt before cooking. Vegetables eaten raw in a salad require salad dressing; cooked vegetables also need flavor added for full enjoyment.

Today there are so many flavored Balsamic vinegars on the market. Depending on what the vinegars are made from, the taste and strength vary. This is why you want to taste as you go; start with less of all ingredients until you reach the desired flavor. Stevia can be either powdered or liquid (I prefer powdered), Celtic Grey Sea Salt is supposedly the best, and ideally the water is filtered. There are times when I don't want as much flavor as is provided by vinegar, so I use instead:

Tomato Sauce OR Chicken Broth OR Beef Broth
Stevia (less than vinegar or none with broth)
Celtic Grey Sea Salt
Water

I urge the reader to experiment and be creative while cooking. Any recipe you find that looks interesting but contains food you choose not to eat, substitute. Stevia sweetens; vinegar, tomato sauce, and broth add flavor and liquid; and brown rice flour adds thickening. Look at a recipe for sweetness, dry ingredients, and liquid ingredients. It only takes practice.

# CHAPTER

# RECIPES

## VEGETABLES

## CAULIFLOWER MASHED POTATOES

NOTE: You will need a large food processor with knife blade for this recipe to have the consistency and flavor of white mashed potatoes.

INGREDIENTS:

1-2 heads Cauliflower
Earth Balance Margarine or Butter
Onion Powder
Garlic Powder
Salt to taste

Unsweetened Almond Milk only if consistency is too thick.

- Wash cauliflower.
- Break the flower sections apart before cooking.
- Cook them completely until they are tender and a fork comes out easily. This can be accomplished by either boiling them in water on top of the stove or steaming them in the microwave.
- For the microwave, place the top sections of the cauliflower in a large Pyrex baking dish and fill the bottom with about ¼

cup water. Cover the dish with plastic wrap (Cling Wrap) and leave a corner not covered so steam can escape.

- Place in the microwave and cook it on "high" for about 12-15 minutes or until it is <u>completely</u> cooked.
- Pierce with a fork; the fork should come out of the cauliflower very easily.
- After it is completely cooked, drain all the water off.
- Add the drained cauliflower to the food processor with the knife blade. I add salt, ~1/3 tub of Earth Balance margarine or 1/2 butter; add ~2 Tablespoons of Onion Powder and 1-2 teaspoons Garlic Powder (optional).
- Press "process" key on food processor. If more liquid is needed (which is very rare,) add a very small amount of Almond Milk. Process the cauliflower until it is the consistency of mashed potatoes.

YIELDS 4-8 servings, depending on how much cauliflower you use.

## SWEET SOUR KALE

NOTE: This has the same flavor as Sweet Sour Spinach. It is cooked a bit differently as explained below.

INGREDIENTS:

2-3 Tablespoons Balsamic Vinegar of Modena (red color)
~1 Tablespoon Powdered Stevia
1 Tablespoon Celtic Sea Salt
Water
2 batches Kale, chopped into bite sizes
2 large Purple Onions, chopped

Before you plug in or pre-heat the wok, follow the basic steps listed below:

- Wash Kale thoroughly and cut into bite sizes.
- Peel and chop onions.
- Place vegetables into two serving bowls. (The chopped kale and chopped onion together should fill two serving bowls). Set them beside the cold wok.
- In a 2-cup Pyrex pouring cup with a handle, place 2-3 Tablespoons vinegar (my favorite is Balsamic of Modena) into the bottom; then add powered stevia (~1 Tablespoon) on top of the vinegar; add 1 Tablespoon of Light Grey Celtic sea salt.
- Fill the rest of the cup with water and stir.
- Place into microwave. Heat on high for about 2 minutes. This makes stirring all ingredients together more efficient. It also saves cooking time in the long run.
- Taste the liquid. If it needs salt, stevia, or vinegar, add a small amount and stir. Taste again. If your vinegar or other ingredients are too strong, dilute by adding water. Make certain this mixture is to your liking <u>before</u> you go any further following this recipe.
- Stir completely and set beside the wok.
- Get out a bottle of Olive Oil, remove the top, and place it beside the cold, unplugged wok.
- Turn the wok on to 300°F. Within 30 seconds, hold your hand about six inches over the bottom to feel it is heating. It will start to heat immediately.
- As soon as you can feel the heat, pour the oil into the bottom of the wok.
- For most recipes, place all the vegetables at one time into the wok.

- Stir vegetables until they are all covered with oil and begin to cook.
- Pour the pre-heated contents contained in the 2-cup Pyrex pouring cup over the vegetables. If more water is needed, add it now and stir vegetables completely.
- Place the lid on the wok.
- Turn the wok up on highest setting, only until the liquid begins to boil. Once is does, turn it down to about 250-300°F and cook until a fork can easily slip through the vegetables.
- Kale takes a very long time to cook (~20-25 minutes), or test the firmness with a fork.

YIELDS 6-8 servings

---

# SWEET SOUR SPINACH

INGREDIENTS:

2-3 Tablespoons Balsamic Vinegar of Modena (red color)
~1 Tablespoon Powdered Stevia
1 Tablespoon Celtic Sea Salt
Water
2 largest, plastic tubs of
Organic Girl Baby Spinach, Washed 3 times
2 Purple Onions, chopped
Olive Oil

Before you plug in or pre-heat the wok, follow the steps below:

- Have the onions chopped and ready to place into the wok. Open both tubs of spinach and set beside the wok.
- In a 2-cup Pyrex pouring cup with a handle, pour into cup the vinegar; add powered stevia on top of the vinegar; add Light Grey Celtic sea salt.
- Fill the rest of the cup with water and stir.
- Place into microwave. Heat on high for about 2 minutes. This makes stirring the ingredients together more efficient. It also saves cooking time in the long run.
- Stir completely and set beside the wok.
- Get out a bottle of Olive Oil, remove the top, and place it beside the cold, unplugged wok.
- Turn the wok on to 350°F. Within 30 seconds, hold your hand about six inches over the bottom to feel if it is heating. It will start to heat immediately.
- As soon as you can feel the heat, pour the oil into the bottom of the wok.
- First place the chopped onions into the wok with oil. Stir well. Place lid on and cook 1-2 minutes.
- Remove lid and add 1 tub of spinach. Stir onion up from the bottom and get oil over the spinach and onions.
- Place lid on top of wok. Let this first tub of spinach cook down for several minutes.
- Lift lid and stir spinach with onions.
- Add second tub of spinach.
- Pour the pre-heated contents contained in the 2-cup Pyrex pouring cup over the vegetables. If more water is needed; add another cup of water and stir completely.
- Place the lid on the wok.

- Turn the wok up on highest setting until the liquid begins to boil. Once is does, turn it down to about 300°F and cook until a fork can easily slip through the vegetables. The time you cook them depends on whether you like them "al-dente" or fully cooked. Fully cooked spinach takes about ten minutes.

YIELDS 6-8 servings

---

# ZUCCHINI ITALIAN STYLE

## INGREDIENTS:

1 Can Tomato Sauce (28 ounces/1 pound 12 ounces)
1 teaspoon (or less) Powdered Stevia
1 Tablespoon Celtic Sea Salt
Water
6-8 Large Zucchini Squash and/or Yellow Neck Squash
2 Purple Onions, chopped
Garlic Powder (granulated) to taste
Basil (~1-2 Tablespoons) or to taste
Parsley (~1-2 Tablespoons) or to taste
Oregano (~1-2 teaspoons) or to taste
Olive Oil

- Have the Squash and Onions chopped, placed into the serving bowls and set beside the cold wok. The wok will hold two large serving bowls of chopped vegetables.
- In a 2-cup Pyrex pouring cup with a handle, pour the tomato sauce; add powered stevia on top of the sauce; add Light Grey Celtic sea salt.

- Place into microwave. Heat on high for about two minutes. This makes stirring the liquid and dry ingredients together more efficient and saves cooking time.
- Stir completely and set beside the wok.
- Get out bottle of Olive Oil, remove the top, and place it beside the cold, unplugged wok.
- Turn the wok on to 300°-350°F. Within 30 seconds, hold your hand about six inches over the bottom to feel it is heating. It will start to heat almost immediately.
- As soon as you can feel the heat, pour the oil into the bottom of the wok.
- Place all chopped vegetables into the wok and stir well until all vegetables are covered with the pre-heated olive oil.
- Sprinkle the vegetables with the desired amounts of herbs (Basil, Parsley, Oregano, and any other of your favorite Italian herbs) and Powdered Garlic.
- Stir completely.
- Pour the contents of the 2-cup Pyrex pouring cup over the vegetables. If more water is needed; add another cup of water and stir completely.
- Place the lid on the wok.
- Turn the wok up on highest setting until the liquid begins to boil. Once is does, turn it down to about 300°F or less, and cook until a fork can easily slip through the vegetables. The time you cook it depends on whether you like them "al-dente" or fully cooked. Fully cooked takes approximately 20 minutes.

YIELDS: 4-6 servings

# CHICKEN

NOTE: I believe all recipes are simply ideas of various food combinations and flavors. I have discussed how I cook vegetables and why I use a wok in which to cook them. Since I have always liked creamy, sweet food like ice cream, I have created some chicken recipes which will give you that type of taste and texture with chicken and gravy instead of sugary desserts. Stevia is 400 times the strength of sugar, so very little is needed to achieve sweetness in a recipe.

## CREAMY FIGGY CHICKEN

You will need a 12-inch skillet with a tight fitting lid and a 2-cup Pyrex Pouring Cup. Preheat skillet to medium-low.

INGREDIENTS:

Fig Balsamic Vinegar (Harvest Hill) ~ 1/4 – 1/3 cup
Stevia, powdered ~ 2-3 teaspoons (to taste)
Celtic Grey Sea Salt ~1 teaspoon
4 large, skinless Chicken Breasts
Finely granulated sea salt (Hain)
Garlic Powder (granulated)
Brown Rice Flour
Olive Oil

- Preheat skillet on low or medium low setting.
- Pour vinegar into 2-cup Pyrex pouring cup.
- Place powdered Stevia on top.
- Add Celtic Grey Sea Salt.
- Fill with water to the 2-cup line.

- Place in microwave and cook 2 minutes on high.
- Set beside the skillet.
- Taste the mixture. If you need more vinegar, stevia, or salt, add it. If you have too strong a flavor of any ingredient for your taste pour some of the liquid out and add some water to make it less strong. Do not continue until you are happy with the flavor of this liquid as it is the key to the recipe. The cooked version will be a little less strong than the liquid.
- Thoroughly rinse and drain the chicken breasts and place them on a chopping board or very large plate.
- They need to be damp to retain the brown rice flour, but not too wet because water added to hot oil will splash hot oil out of the skillet and could burn you.
- Season the chicken breasts with Hain, finely granulated sea salt and garlic powder (granulated).
- Completely cover and work the brown rice flour into the chicken breasts on both sides. The easiest way to do this is to place them in a paper or plastic bag with the brown rice flour. Tightly close the paper bag or seal the plastic bag. Turn the bag in all directions so that the chicken breasts are completely covered with the flour.
- Pour olive oil into preheated skillet.
- The burner setting should be on medium-low.
- Use tongs to retrieve the chicken from the bag and place each breast into the oil. The oil should be hot enough to brown the chicken, but if it is too hot the chicken will burn.
- Set timer for 2 minutes.

- Cook 2 minutes; turn breasts over and cook another 1 minute. They should be browned, but not dark brown. Keep your burner on medium-low.
- When the timer goes off, pour liquid into skillet and cover. Cook another 6 minutes.
- Remove lid; take a sharp knife and fork to slice into a breast to see if it is done. If it is rare in the middle, turn the breasts over and cook 2-3 more minutes; check again with a knife and fork.
- You don't want it to be rare; however when it is very slightly pink you can put the lid back onto the skillet and remove it from the heat. The cooking time also depends on the thickness of the breasts. Once you see the inside is pink, do not cook it longer than 1 minute. Set a timer!
- Overcooking chicken breasts will make them tough.
- The liquid and the brown rice flour will combine with the oil to make gravy while cooking.
- After you have removed the cooked breasts from the skillet, slice them into bite-sized pieces and put them on a plate.
- Stir remaining gravy in the pan and spoon over the breasts before serving.

YIELDS 4 servings

---

# CREAMY LEMON CHICKEN

You will need a 12-inch skillet with a tight fitting lid and a 2-cup Pyrex pouring cup. Preheat skillet to medium-low.

INGREDIENTS:

The juice of one-half a fresh lemon

Stevia, powdered, ~ 1 teaspoon or less

4 large, skinless Chicken Breasts

Finely granulated Sea Salt (Hain)

Garlic Powder (granulated)

Brown Rice Flour

Olive Oil

- Pour lemon juice into Pyrex cup.
- Place powdered Stevia on top.
- Add ~1/2 teaspoon or less sea salt. (optional) Keep in mind that you are going to season the chicken with salt, so it depends on your taste.
- Fill with water to the 2-cup line.
- Place in microwave and cook 2 minutes on high.
- Remove and stir thoroughly.
- Set beside the skillet.
- Preheat skillet on low or medium-low.
- Thoroughly rinse and drain chicken breasts and place them on a chopping board or very large plate.
- They need to be damp to retain the brown rice flour, but not too wet.
- Season with salt and garlic powder (granulated).
- Completely cover and work the brown rice flour into the chicken breasts on both sides. The easiest way to do this is to place them in a paper or plastic bag with the flour. Tightly close the paper bag or seal the plastic bag. Turn the bag in all directions so that the chicken breasts are completely covered with the flour.
- Pour olive oil into preheated skillet.
- Place the floured chicken breasts into the oil.

- Set timer for 2 minutes.
- When the timer goes off, turn breasts over and cook another 1 minute. They should be browned, but not dark brown. Keep the burner on medium-low.
- Pour liquid into skillet and cover. Cook another 6 minutes.
- Remove lid; take a sharp knife and fork and slice into a breast to see if it is done. You don't want it to be rare meat; however if it is pink, you can cook 1 more minute. If it is very slightly pink, remove skillet from heat and set aside. Let it rest for a few minutes.
- Overcooking chicken breasts will make them tough.
- The liquid and the brown rice flour will combine with the oil to make gravy while cooking.
- After you have removed the cooked breasts from the skillet, place them on a chopping board. Slice them into bite-sized pieces and put them on a plate.
- Stir remaining gravy in the pan and spoon over the breasts before serving.

YIELDS 4 servings

## CREAMY CHICKEN IDEAS

Follow all instructions from the Creamy Figgy Chicken recipe by using your favorite flavored Balsamic or other vinegar. As you can see the flavor comes from either the vinegar or the lemon juice. Both are tart and full of flavor. The Stevia will counteract the tartness to give you a sweet-sour type of flavor.

My favorite vinegars are:

- Balsamic of Modena
- Golden Balsamic of Modena
- Fig Balsamic by Harvest Hill
- Peach Balsamic by Harvest Hill

If you want creamed chicken with simple gravy, use chicken broth (salted) without any stevia.

# BEEF

NOTE: The following Beef Stew is the basic recipe that can be turned into your favorite Chili or Italian Stew recipe. Using the substitution method, you can make this recipe into whatever flavor you want by adding different herbs and spices. I have tried many different ways in which to flavor this recipe, but the following is the one that has become a staple over the years.

## BEEF STEW

INGREDIENTS:

1 bunch Celery
2 large Purple Onions or your favorite onions
Basil
Parsley
Stevia
Sea Salt (Hain granulated)
Garlic Powder (granulated)
1 (28 ounces) can Tomato Sauce or Crushed Tomatoes
2 (14.5 ounces/411g) cans Diced Tomatoes, Fire Roasted
2 Pounds Ground Beef

Olive Oil

Pre-heat the skillet to low/medium-low setting.

- Wash and prepare celery for slicing. The best way to get the strings out is to have the celery stalk with the curly side facing upwards (as though you were going to stuff the stalk with almond butter and eat raw). Take a sharp knife and touch each end of the stalk so you can lift up one end at a time, pulling the strings towards the other end. Repeat this process from the other end of the stalk. This will remove most of the strings. Finally, touch the middle of the stalk with a sharp knife and pull the strings down to each end.
- After you have removed the strings, cut small slices (crosswise) until all the stalks are chopped into small pieces. If you have a slicer blade on your food processor, this is a perfect opportunity to use it.
- Pour olive oil into pre-heated skillet to completely cover the skillet.
- Add sliced celery.
- Add herbs, sprinkle with salt and garlic powder. Stir completely and place lid on skillet.
- While the celery is cooking, chop the onions into pieces similar in size to the celery pieces.
- Once the onions are chopped, check the celery to make certain it is becoming tender.
- Once the celery is almost cooked, add chopped onions and stir completely.
- You may need to add more olive oil as the celery absorbs it more than most vegetables.
- Place lid on skillet and cook celery and onions until onions turn clear.

- Pour entire contents of skillet into a large 8-quart stewpot. Set the stewpot on another burner and turn it on "low" while you are preparing the ground beef.
- Place ground beef onto a chopping board. Press it down to make a one-half inch thick slab of raw meat.

NOTE: *To make this task easier, first place the ground beef into the food processor with the knife blade and process. This makes the raw beef more tender and the slicing of it easier.*

- With your largest, sharpest knife, cut the slab crosswise and then lengthwise to create small bite sized pieces. These pieces will cook evenly and the sizes will be compatible with the sizes of the other ingredients in the stew.
- Add enough olive oil to cover the bottom of the skillet.
- Add the pieces of ground beef to the skillet.
- With a spatula, stir the beef pieces until they are about half browned.
- Place the cooked beef pieces into the stewpot with the other ingredients.
- Add the tomato sauce and diced tomatoes. Sprinkle a small amount of powdered stevia on top of the tomato mixture. This will bring out the flavor of the tomato.
- Stir all ingredients in the stewpot
- Turn the burner high enough and cook until the mixture begins to slightly boil.
- After it begins to boil, turn down burner.
- Cover stewpot and cook about 15-30 minutes. Stir to make sure it doesn't stick to the bottom of the stewpot. Do not overcook as this will make the beef dry.

NOTE: I have used this basic recipe in the crockpot; however I did not use raw celery. Instead I added a package of organic sweet peas. I have found that while the crockpot is quick and easy to assemble, the raw ground meat will cook together and be difficult to slice into bite sized pieces when it has finished cooking. It will also be dry and be less flavorful. I've not had great success with crockpot cooking as others I know have had. If you have, then you know what to do.

YIELD: 6-8 servings

# FILET MIGNON

Preheat Oven to 425°F.

Preheat skillet to medium or medium-low. You want it hot enough to sear the meat, not burn it.

INGREDIENTS:

2 Beef Filet Mignon Steaks
Hain Sea Salt
Garlic Powder (granulated)
Olive Oil
When skillet and oven are preheated

- Season steaks with Salt and granulated Garlic Powder.
- Pour enough Olive Oil into the skillet to just cover the bottom.
- Place each filet (serving side down) into the skillet. Place lid on skillet.
- Set timer for 2 minutes.
- Turn the steaks over and set the timer for 2 minutes. Place lid on skillet.

- When timer goes off, place skillet with lid on into the preheated, 425°F oven. If you want the inside to be rare, cook it for 6 minutes. If you want it to be medium-rare, cook for 7 minutes. If you want it medium cook for 8 minutes.
- When you remove the skillet from the oven, make certain you use heavy oven mittens to handle the skillet. Keep those oven mittens close so you won't accidently touch any part of the skillet with your bare hands (this is experience speaking).
- You can serve them whole, or slice them into bite-sized portions.
- Cover the cooked meat with the remaining Olive Oil and drippings from the skillet. Use a large spoon to stir the Olive Oil together with the drippings and spoon over cooked meat before serving.

YIELD 2 servings

# MEAT BALLS AND SPAGHETTI

This is an example of how you can substitute ingredients for any Meat Ball and Spaghetti recipe to make it gluten free and very low in carbohydrates. Make your favorite meal ball recipe, except substitute brown rice flour for bread crumbs.

MEAT BALLS

INGREDIENTS:

2 pounds free-range Ground Beef
2 Purple Onions, sliced in large pieces
Sea Salt (Hain)
Brown Rice Flour

2 Eggs

Basil ~ 2 Tablespoons

Parsley ~ 2 Tablespoons

Oregano ~ 2 teaspoons

Garlic, crushed, diced or granulated powder

Tomato Paste ~3 Tablespoons

Stevia ~1/2 teaspoon

- Add sliced onions to food processor and process until the onions are in very small pieces.
- Take several handfuls of ground meat and add to processor.
- Add salt to taste, basil, parsley, oregano, and garlic. Process.
- Add more small handfuls of ground meat and process.
- Add eggs and brown rice flour, tomato paste, and stevia. Process.
- Continue to slowly add ingredients and process until completely combined and the proper consistency is reached.
- I use a very small ice-cream scoop to remove them from the food processor.
- Drop each raw meat ball into a stewpot with boiling water, or fry them in a skillet with olive oil.
- Remove them with a slotted spoon when they are firm enough to do so.
- Place them into the Marinara Sauce to finish cooking.

## MARINARA SAUCE

## INGREDIENTS:

Tomato Sauce 2 cans (28-ounces)

Stevia 1/2 teaspoon

Basil ~2 Tablespoons

Parsley ~2 Tablespoons

Oregano ~2 teaspoons

Anise or Fennel ~1 Tablespoon (optional)

- Combine above ingredients together in a large pot.
- Warm it so it will be ready to receive meatballs when they come out of the boiling water.
- Cook meatballs on low (or in a crockpot) in Marinara sauce until they are done.

## SPAGHETTI SQUASH

- Wash squash and pat dry.
- Cut the squash in half crosswise.
- Remove seeds with spoon or fork.
- Place into microwaveable dish, flesh down.
- Cover with Cling Wrap; leave a corner for steam to escape.
- Put 1/4 cup water into dish.
- Place in microwave for 15 minutes on high setting.
- When cooked completely, set aside, remove Cling Wrap and let steam leave pan.
- Use heavy oven mittens as they will be extremely hot.
- With a fork, remove cooked squash by 'raking' the fork over the flesh.

This is a very low carbohydrate and gluten free substitute for noodles.

# PORK

## BONELESS PORK LOIN ROAST

Preheat oven to 325°F. You will need a 12-inch skillet with a tight fitting lid that can be placed into a 325°F oven for 55 minutes. I use a stainless steel skillet with a lid.

INGREDIENTS:

2 ½ pound Boneless Pork Loin Roast
Finely granulated Sea Salt (Hain)
Brown Rice Flour
3/4 cup filtered water in a pouring cup
Olive Oil

- Preheat skillet on medium or medium-low burner.
- Remove roast from its packaging and rinse it thoroughly.
- You want it damp so it will retain the flour, but not wet as you are going to brown it in hot oil.
- Cut the roast in half crosswise because of the size of the roast and skillet.
- Season with salt. Use any other herbs or spices at this time if you wish.
- Completely cover and rub brown rice flour into the roast on all sides.
- Place your hand 6 inches over the warming skillet to see if it is hot enough for browning.
- Once it is warm enough, pour olive oil into the skillet to just cover the entire bottom.

- If you have a long-tong type fork that comes with a knife set, use it. If not use a fork with the longest tongs you have.
- Pick up each half of the roast, one at a time, and place each into the olive oil in the skillet.
- Brown for 1 minute (just lightly browned) on all sides (this includes the ends).
- Pour the water into the skillet.
- Place the lid on the skillet.
- Place it all into the pre-heated oven.
- Set a timer for 55 minutes.
- After the timer goes off, get a very thick towel or oven mitt and remove the skillet from the oven and set it on top of the cold cook top.
- Remove the lid with a thick towel or oven mitt.
- With a very sharp, long carving knife, cut each piece in half.
- If the roast is slightly pink, with a thick oven mitt, place the lid back onto the skillet and let it rest for about 5 minutes.
- If the roast is very pink, put it back into the oven for no more than 2 minutes.

NOTE: The key to a tender pork roast is to not overcook it. It will continue to cook while resting.

- When the roast is done, slice it, and cut the slices into bite sized pieces.
- Place pieces onto a plate.
- Cover the pieces with the juice remaining in the skillet.

YIELD: 4 servings

# DEVILED HAM

You will need a large food processor with a knife blade.

INGREDIENTS:

- American Homestead Boneless Pork Ham Steak or equivalent. (~1 pound, more or less)
- Eden brand Organic Brown Mustard, Stone Ground with Apple Cider vinegar. (This is the only very strong, spicy mustard I have found that does not contain sugar.)
- Stevia – 1/2 teaspoon or less
- Onion Powder – 1-2 Tablespoons
- Mayonnaise

PREPARATION:

- Remove skin from ham.
- Cut into chunks ~2 inches square.
- Place into food processor and press "process."
- Add 2 Tablespoons mustard, stevia, onion powder and mayonnaise.
- Process until desired consistency is reached.

This is an excellent ham salad mix that goes well on top sliced avocado or your favorite raw vegetables. Cover with roasted pecan halves (or pieces) to add crunch to this very creamy recipe. Another version is to add very small pieces of sliced Baked apples, see Page 75.

YIELD: 3-4 servings

# MISCELLANEOUS RECIPES

## BAKED APPLES
### (AS A CONDIMENT)

You will need a Pyrex dish (11-cup rectangular), a very sharp paring knife, a chopping board, and Cling Wrap. This is a microwave recipe.

INGREDIENTS:

5-6 SMALL APPLES, washed
Stevia powdered
Cinnamon finely ground

- Place an apple with stem up.
- Slice in half.
- Place half apple flesh down.
- Slice in half.
- Take other half, flesh down and slice in half.
- Take each quarter, flesh up, and slice in half.
- You should have 8 pieces of apple.
- Peel each slice.
- Once peeled, place them in rows in the bottom of the Pyrex dish.
- When you get one layer, sprinkle with powdered stevia and sprinkle with cinnamon.
- Repeat process and create a layer of sliced apples on top of the first.
- Sprinkle top layer with powdered stevia and ground cinnamon.

- Cover with Cling Wrap, leaving a large corner open for the steam to escape. Add 2-3 Tablespoons water to the dish through the opening.
- Place in microwave and cook on high for 12 minutes.
- When finished cooking, remove from microwave with heavy oven mitts.
- Place on safe surface to cool.
- Remove Cling Wrap immediately.
- This is best served cold. I keep a batch in the refrigerator to use as condiments in various ways.

I only eat 4-6 slices a day, and not every day. I cut each slice into about 6 small pieces and use them like raisins in recipes. These small pieces can be stirred into the Deviled Ham recipe. The whole slices can be served as a condiment with Boneless Pork Loin Roast.

YIELD: However you use the baked apples!

---

# SALAD DRESSING

You can use any oil and vinegar recipe you might know or find preprinted. A salad dressing is a perfect way in which to get brain-healthy oils like Olive, Avocado, Walnut, and Almond. Any flavor vinegar will do. Simply use your favorite.

## GARLIC SALAD DRESSING

INGREDIENTS:

2 parts Olive Oil
1 part Red Wine or Balsamic Vinegar

2 teaspoons crushed garlic (to taste)

Salt (to taste)

Stevia (to taste)

- Place all ingredients into a blender.
- Cover and blend until smooth.
- Taste as you go to get desired flavor.

YIELD: However much you need.

# YAMS OR SWEET POTATOES

## (MADE TO TASTE LIKE PUMPKIN PIE)

You will need a 6 or 8-quart stewpot with colander and either a food processor with knife blade or electric mixer.

INGREDIENTS:

4-6 Jewel Yams or Sweet Potatoes

Finely ground Cinnamon (to taste)

1/2 tub Earth Balance Margarine

Stevia (very little – taste as you go)

- Peel Yams.
- Cut crosswise (into about 4 or 5 pieces each) and place into stewpot (without colander).
- Fill with water to 2 inches below top of pot.
- Boil until they are completely cooked – check each piece until a fork easily slips through the flesh. This is very important.
- When cooked, drain well.

- Immediately put into very large mixing bowl or very large food processor with knife blade.
- Add margarine, cinnamon and stevia. Mix completely or "process."
- They can be served hot or cold.
- I like them cold because they have more flavor than when they are hot.
- I eat a serving instead of my brown rice serving, or on days when I do not use brown rice flour for cooking.

YIELDS 8-10 servings

# DESSERT

In parting I sincerely hope this book will be a helpful guide to anyone who chooses to use it. I had the energy and mental acuity to write it at age sixty-seven because I followed the eating strategy contained within it for more than seven years. After fighting my weight for more than fifty years, I can assure you that this is the only eating strategy I've ever tried that really works. I did not do a formal work out at the gym; I took care of a home and fed two people fresh food, three times a day. It is the simplest, easiest, and fastest way to nourish your body while the pounds melt away and you reach whatever size you want to be.

I had incentive to continue to stay on this eating plan after my first bout with Mycological Syndrome because I was losing weight effortlessly, had more mental acuity and overall energy than I had had in years. Not only did I recover from sugar addiction, I came to detest it which is why I consider myself to be a recovered sugar addict. The over-use of this one substance took me dangerously close to having insulin-dependent Type II Diabetes. To date it has prevented me from developing Dementia

(Type III Diabetes). I am able to stand, cook, and walk small distances instead of spending my life in a wheel chair. Thankfully I have not lost my personal power, nor do I feel invisible in public.

Nothing I have ever eaten in my entire life tasted good enough to be worth the years of struggle and pain I have endured. Food is fuel for the body; not a form of recreation. Food can be as delicious as it is nutritious. As a nation, the large amount of junk food we eat is making us fat and sick. It is my hope that this book will inspire and teach the younger generations how to cook and eat before their weight becomes out of control. If you are an overweight young person, now is the time to begin a new way of thinking and eating to become or stay slim. Everyone needs this skill because everyone needs to eat. No one needs to live in an obese body. It is a matter of choice, commitment to that choice, and prioritizing your time to achieve the goals you set for yourself. You and only you decide what you eat; you are the master of your destiny; and you (and your loved ones) pay the price or reap the benefit in the future for the choices you make today.

*"Whatever you can do, or dream you can do,*
*begin it.*
*Boldness has genius, power, and magic in it.*
*Begin it now!"*

GOETHE

-END-